listen!
knowing the world and fighting to change it

scott Neigh

fernwood publishing
halifax & winnipeg

Copyright 2025 © Scott Neigh.

All rights reserved. No part of this book may be reproduced or transmitted in any form by any means without permission in writing from the publisher, except by a reviewer, who may quote brief passages in a review. The publisher expressly prohibits the use of this work in connection with the development of any software program, including, without limitation, training a machine learning or generative artificial intelligence (AI) system.

Development editor: Errol Sharpe
Copyediting and text design: Brenda Conroy
Cover design: Amanda Priebe
Typeface for title/author: Lineal by Frank Adebiaye, with the contribution of Anton Moglia, Ariel Martín Pérez. Distributed by velvetyne.fr.
Printed and bound in the UK

Published by Fernwood Publishing
Halifax and Winnipeg
2970 Oxford Street, Halifax, Nova Scotia, B3L 2W4
www.fernwoodpublishing.ca

Fernwood Publishing Company Limited gratefully acknowledges the financial support of the Government of Canada through the Canada Book Fund and the Canada Council for the Arts. We acknowledge the Province of Manitoba for support through the Manitoba Publishers Marketing Assistance Program and the Book Publishing Tax Credit. We acknowledge the Nova Scotia Department of Communities, Culture and Heritage for support through the Publishers Assistance Fund.

Library and Archives Canada Cataloguing in Publication
Title: Listen! : knowing the world and fighting to change it / Scott Neigh.
Names: Neigh, Scott, author
Description: Includes bibliographical references and index.
Identifiers: Canadiana 20250252341 | ISBN 9781773637563 (softcover)
Subjects: LCSH: Listening. | LCSH: Listening—Social aspects. | LCSH: Activism. | LCSH: Social movements. | LCSH: Social change.
Classification: LCC BF323.L5 N45 2025 | DDC 153.6/8—dc23

contents

acknowledgements v

introduction: listening, social movements, and this book 1
    listening matters 2
    movements 6
    the path to this book 7
    this book's approach 9

part 1: what listening is

1 listening practices 14
    not hearing, but listening 15
    noticing and attention 17
    listening practices 19
    listening is learned 22
    listening brings the social world inside of you 25

2 listening to each other 29
    what we say about listening 29
    listening is more than an individual act 32
    how voices reach us 33
    how voices matter 34
    listening and making change 36
    listening requires other people 38

3 listening weaves the world 39
    our experience 40
    complexity, reification, liberalism, and individualism 42
    other accounts of the social 46
    dealing with multiplicity 48
    grounding in experience 50
    characteristics of the world 52
    keeping people at the centre 55
    the social world and listening 58

part 2: listening's reach and limits

4 the scream and the murmur 60
    listening in practice   62
    conversation   65
    what i hear   67

5 failures and harms 72
    listening is not enough   72
    harm shapes our listening   74
    listening and harm   78
    listening's failures and harms are socially produced   82
    thinking of power in terms of listening   86

part 3: listening and change

6 everyday resistance 90
    orienting to moments   91
    weapons of the weak   94
    more everyday resistance   97
    in the context of relations   101
    what everyday resistance is and what it isn't   105

7 collective movements 107
    beyond everyday resistance   107
    collectivity and reconfigured relationships   110
    the work of resistance   113
    the work of listening   116
    listening between movements   118
    listening and the harms of movements   121

8 learning from movements 126
    listening to everyday and movement struggle   131
    evaluating what we hear from movements   136
    kinds of movement knowledge   139
    the limits remain   143

conclusion: listening shapes movements, movements shape listening 144

epilogue 148

notes 153

index 173

acknowledgements

The older I get, the greater the number of people who deserve thanks for making me who I am and for enabling the work that I do. A sad consequence of this is, perhaps paradoxically, that I can thank far fewer of the deserving people by name than I did in the books I published in 2012.

The thinking that became this book emerged from *Talking Radical Radio,* the weekly radio show and podcast I started working on not too long after those books came out. This book does not directly draw on the more than five hundred in-depth interviews with activists and organizers that I did for the show, but nonetheless it is very much a consequence of the countless hours of listening and reflecting I did as part of that work. Unfortunately, it would not be practical to name everyone who shared their stories with me, let alone everyone who made suggestions about who to interview and all the people at community radio stations and online progressive media outlets who made the show what it was, but I am grateful to all of you.

Thank-you to Chris Dixon, Candida Hadley, and Stacey Ritz for offering valuable feedback on the manuscript. As well, though we get to see much less of each other than we did in those long-ago days when we lived, worked, and organized in the same city, an additional thank-you to Chris for his support and encouragement and for the opportunity for ongoing engagement with someone of similar sensibilities who does similar work.

I extend a particular thank-you to Gary Kinsman. Writing this book helped me appreciate how much I learned and how much my thinking was shaped by the years I spent doing grassroots political work with him in Sudbury, Ontario. I don't necessarily apply any of it in the ways that he would — readers should blame me for the bits they disagree with, not anyone else — but some of that influence can be seen in the use I make of work by Dorothy Smith and some broader aspects of how I talk about the social world, in my use of John Holloway's idea of "the scream" in Chapter 4, in much of what I say about knowledge produced in and by social movements in Chapter 8, and in lots of other things too. Thank-you, Gary!

Thank-you to Jennifer Johnson for the intensive one-on-one reading course we did many years ago, which at the time I intended to use as a basis for my next book, even though the meandering path of my writing process has taken me to a place that has absolutely nothing to do with what we read together that summer. Thank-you to Mrinalini Greedharry for the ongoing conversation despite how far apart we live these days — I have probably talked more about writing with you than with anyone else over the last decade, and your steadfast care and support have meant a great deal to me, in this area as in so many others. Thank-you to the people I have done grassroots political work with over the years, from my earliest activism in the 1990s to my more recent emphasis on movement infrastructure — these experiences of working collectively to make change shaped the words in these pages. Thank-you to the dear people across various facets of my life who, in the face of my impulse towards solitude and quiet, persist in giving me opportunities to listen, to learn, sometimes to speak, sometimes to think together, sometimes to play, to connect, and to just generally be in relation. I don't always make it easy, but I value you!

Thank-you to Errol Sharpe, Jazz Cook, Anumeha Gokhale, Lauren Jeanneau, Art Bouman, Beverley Rach, Brenda Conroy, Amanda Priebe, and the rest of the Fernwood team for giving me the opportunity to share this book with the world and for making it far better than I could have managed on my own.

Thank-you to the feline companions who have graced me with their company through many solitary workdays and thereby eased the frustration that sometimes accompanies any effort to turn blank page or screen into something worth reading — Charlie, who left us as this project approached completion, and Meabh and Una, who more recently joined us. Thank-you, most of all, to Stacey Ritz and Liam Ritz Neigh for their constant love, support, and understanding. Without the two of you, none of what I do would be possible.

introduction

listening, social movements, and this book

This book begins from an inadequate epiphany. I had just finished listening to a recording of an interview I had done with a participant in a movement for social justice. Unfortunately, I no longer remember who it was or what we talked about, though I clearly remember the feel of it, the room I was in, and the vista of snow blanketing an inelegant northern Ontario mishmash of laneway, scrubby trees, and asphalt stretching beneath my window. It was a slow listening, a careful listening — a listening in which the words swirled around me, bubbled, stewed, carried me through events, projected implications about the larger world that had moulded the circumstances they described. It was a moment of listening that was unique, shaped by the words that one person had shared about their life and about their work with others to make change. But it also evoked my experience of hundreds of other such encounters, each conveying unique selves, struggles, and insights into the world.

It was this juxtaposition of singularity with so many echoes that sparked my epiphany. I caught a breathtaking view of the breadth and power of the words of our neighbours, of the people across town, of people around the world. If we listened — truly listened — to their words, to the shape of their everyday lives, to the realities of and knowledge generated in their struggles both individual and collective, we could transform the world. If we listened, truly listened, how could we not hear the urgency of radically re-making a world that organizes harm, violence, and death into so many lives? And if we listened, truly listened, these many disparate glimpses into the *what* of the world, and the *how,* could give us the seeds of the knowledge we need to begin making that change.

Soon enough, the feeling of certainty and completeness that comes with epiphany had faded, and the murk and complexity of reality intruded once more. I knew that things were just not that simple, that my moment of insight was inadequate. I had been involved enough in social movements, and I'd heard enough from others who had done far more than me, to know that change of any substance would not be brought about solely by listening more or better or differently.

There are certainly liberal fantasies in which listening is enough. In these fantasies, injustice is caused by ignorance and can be undone by education, or it is the result of individual badness and can be rectified by moral suasion, exhortation, and example. Certainly, knowledge is bound up in complex and important ways with social injustice and struggles for collective liberation, some of which are touched on in this book. It can also be important to point out the immorality of allowing injustice to thrive. However, injustice is not fundamentally about what is in individual minds or hearts but rather about power and benefit. It is, moreover, about how the world is socially organized, an idea I talk about more in later chapters.

However, as I continued to reflect on it, I could not let go of my sense that listening was central. I decided that while my epiphany might be inadequate, there was still something to it. There *is* something powerful to such listening, to the bringing together of our respective fragments of the social world to better understand the whole, and to acting based on that. There is something vitally important about listening when it comes to how our world works, to how we know the world, and to the collective movements we need to build in order to change it. I just wasn't quite sure what.

listening matters

Almost all of us are listening, almost all the time. Maybe not well, maybe not with any particular understanding, maybe not to what others think we are supposed to or in ways that they expect, but we are listening. Before I say more about that, though, I should probably make clear what I mean by "listening." In colloquial speech, it is common to treat "listening" and "hearing" as closely related in an essential and definitional way, or even to use them interchangeably. However, subtle distinctions exist between them, even in everyday conversation. "Hearing" more often connotes encountering and sensing sound, whereas "listening" at least sometimes implies a certain receptivity to and engagement with what has been heard, an active uptake and attentiveness. For example, I asked my kid to take the recycling out and he heard me, but he didn't listen. Moreover, using "listening" to capture uptake and responsiveness even in the absence of sound is also an entirely unremarkable part of our everyday language. If a friend sends me advice about a difficult situation via text message, it would be perfectly normal, despite its visual form, for my partner to ask, "So are you going to listen to her?"

In this book, I understand "listening" in an expansive way that builds on the non-sense-specific responsiveness that exists within its conventional usage but goes beyond it. Not all of us can hear. Not all of us can see. But most of us take in and respond to the world around us in some way. Sometimes, it is important to name the sensory specifics of how that happens, particularly given how powerfully disabling our world can be to those whose ways of moving through it run counter to dominant expectations and norms. But for a lot of what I talk about here, I think it is often accurate and useful to generalize. So, I use "listening" to encompass all our pathways for taking in, taking up, processing, and actively making sense of the world. If you are Deaf or hearing impaired, if you are neurodivergent — that is, if your brain works differently than what is typical for most people — in a way related to sensory processing, or if your capacities for sensing and making meaning from stimuli differ from dominant norms in any way, you are almost certainly still responsive to and making meaning from the world. I want my language in this book to capture all of that. This is a book not about the auditory but about our overall capacity to be reached by the world, to perceive and respond, to make sense and take action.

In using the word "listening" like this, I am not suggesting that we should start using it in ways that feel weird in how we talk with one another. If you opened your fridge, took out a container of leftover rice, and through how it smelled and looked decided it had gone off and it would be unwise to eat it, you would be unlikely to say that you had listened to the rice. When Dan Aykroyd's character in *Ghostbusters* says, "Listen! You smell something?" it is funny precisely because it is, for most of us,[1] incongruous, silly, nonsensical. But while I am not asking you to change your use of the term, in this book, I mean the word "listening" to capture the experience of taking in and taking up a wide range of sensory inputs rather than just sound. Sometimes, I augment or even replace it with other words explicitly invoking senses other than hearing, but a lot of the time I just say "listening" and trust that you recognize my intention to bring them along. It is the active uptake and attention, the responsiveness, the engagement beyond passive input that I am trying to convey, irrespective of the sensory pathway.

Of course, I could try to find another word to do this, a word without so much sense-specific baggage. Instead of "listening," I could use the more general word "sensing." To me, however, that feels similar to the passive encounter with sensory input implied by "hearing," rather than the uptake and engagement of "listening." I could perhaps find ways to use the language of "paying attention," but as I discuss later, that captures only one element of the many practices we bring together in our listening to the world. I could use a composite phrase, like "sensing and engaging" or "sensing and responding," but that would quickly become cumbersome and off-putting. Plus, it feels further from everyday use than just saying "listening." Beyond that, as I explore in Chapter 1, I think that at least some of the baggage the word "listening" carries with it does some work that I want it to do.

With that expansive understanding in mind, I think it is reasonably safe to claim that for most of us, to be sentient and awake is to be listening. On a certain level at least, we just can't help ourselves. So, when I say that I spend a lot of time listening, it is a pretty trite statement, because who doesn't? I don't spend any more of my time doing it than anybody else, nor do I claim to be any better at it — it is a common point in conventional sources about listening, some of which I touch on in Chapter 2, that most of us think we are much better listeners than we actually are, and I don't want to fall into that trap. When I say that I know listening has been tremendously important in shaping my life, in shaping *me,* it is similarly trite, because it is true of all of us. I just know that because of quirks of personality and accidents of circumstance — particularly the trajectory of my work — I have ended up spending quite a bit of time being deliberate about listening. Because of that, I have had lots of opportunity to think about why it is important, both in our lives as a whole and specifically in the context of struggles for collective liberation.

And when I say that listening matters, I know that is the case because my own life has told me so. I could get all philosophical about it. I could talk about the social flows of doing in and through me[2] and their dependence on our respective responsive capacities. I could talk about language itself and how I would not have the words I have if they had not already been filled with meaning in the mouths of others[3] and then taken in and up by me. There is certainly value to approaching the topic in those ways. But I don't need to do that to feel, deep in my bones, listening's significance. I know just from what I have lived that what I have taken in by ears and eyes and all the rest has shaped who I am today. I don't need psychologists, sociologists, or literary theorists to tell me that what I see and hear, and the meaning I make from it, matter tremendously to my experience of the world and to the *me* that has thus formed. I don't need to wax poetic about the social character of knowledge to be very much aware, every time I sit down to understand the painful events that saturate the news and every time I bring out notebook and pen to jot down some thoughts, how much I owe to my encounters with the experiences and ideas of other people.

Think about the many ways that listening is part of the *how* of life: I don't remember hearing "Don't touch it, it's hot" or "Look both ways" from my mother as a child, but I'm sure I did, and I took in both their obvious lessons and their deeper message of care. I do remember listening to words that did not themselves cause but that nonetheless conveyed irrevocable changes in the course of life — news of a death or pregnancy, "no" to a pitched publication, "yes" to burning hopes of a kiss. I can think of instances of the words of others warmly affirming me or telling me in no uncertain terms how I had screwed up and caused harm, and my complex reactions to both echoing down through subsequent choices. I remember listening to yelling, mostly not directed at me, but shaking me to my core, and it teaching me what I never wanted to be. I remember direct didactic telling by parents and teachers, conversations between adults overheard as a child, lessons unconsciously derived from that which was being assumed and implied on pages and screens. I remember being soothed, troubled, delighted, enlightened, annoyed, and so many other things from listening to the words of co-workers over pints, friends over dinner tables, lovers over pillows. I remember self-medicating downness through blockbusters, fanfiction, and novels I'd read a hundred times already. I remember revelling in listening to the intimate details of other people's lives and relationships. What moment in my life, in your life, in any life has not had its form and flavour touched by listening?

movements

There is more to it than that, though. Yes, listening is something that *I* do and that matters in my life. No doubt the same is true of you. But while we often treat listening solely as something done by individuals, it is in fact much more than that. Listening happens *between* us. It is how we know each other, how we exist in relation with each other, how we can shift from being me, and you, and them to being *we* and acting together. When we listen and come to know things about the world, at least some of the time it is not just a matter of acquiring knowledge like an object to be stored away but of drawing the world into us and being changed by it. When we act in the world, listening both guides us as we do so and is a crucial way in which our actions ripple out as effect — not just others listening to our words, but others observing and responding to our actions.

Because listening is so central to the workings of both our lives and the world writ large, it is also crucial in acting together to make change. When we resist in our everyday lives and when we come together with others to do so in more deliberately collective and self-consciously political ways, listening plays a key role. The ways that our movements form and grow, and the ways that they act and make change, have as much to do with listening as everything else we do. None of the many disparate activities that comprise social movements could happen without us listening to each other and listening to the world. Beyond its role in the *how* of collective struggle, I remember countless actions that, whatever language we used in that moment, boiled down to us telling those with power, "Hey, you aren't listening and that is unjust, so we will make you listen." I remember, also, being told graciously or angrily — or only realizing later via dissecting why something went so wrong — that we were failing to listen in some important way ourselves. I remember countless instances when listening to movements that I am not a part of and the people who comprise them has helped me understand the world better. For all these reasons, I think it is important to think and write about listening and movements not just on their own but together.

Much like my use of "listening," when I talk about "movements," I mean the term broadly. My concern is people working together to make change, however that is happening. This can take many social forms, and the people involved can understand and name what they are doing in a lot of different ways, certainly encompassing social movements as they are conventionally understood but going beyond that. I also use the term "communities-in-struggle" to capture groupings of people who face intense, pervasive oppression and must deal with that together in ongoing ways and who have a collective existence that goes beyond the more fleeting and episodic character of most movements. I leave open my understanding of the forms that collective struggle can take, to be honest about the limits of my knowledge and to allow for surprise and learning.

I am clear, however, that I only mean movements that aim their work towards social justice and collective liberation. As I typed the first draft of this introduction, a movement that was to a certain extent politically eclectic but that had been driven and led by the far right was disrupting the streets of Ottawa, and I most certainly do not mean them.[4] I do not mean any collective effort that appropriates the language of justice but actually seeks to strengthen the social hierarchies at the roots of injustice, unfreedom, and systemic violence — white nationalists, those who support the bosses, those who claim to be pursuing liberation but who actively espouse settler colonialism or hostility to trans people or any other such thing. Those groups are not who I am talking about, or to, in this book.[5]

The movements and other efforts to transform the world that are my focus here are our only hope for a better future. The only way we are ever going to make the change we need is by working collectively to do so. I do not claim to know in detail how that will work, which social forms will be effective, or how the resulting transformed social world will be organized. I am, in fact, deeply suspicious of anyone who claims to have a blueprint, a singular line they insist is true and correct, an analysis that demands our listening but offers none in return. But I do know that the only way we can get there is together.

the path to this book

Within this broader context, it was, as I said, my work over the last two and a half decades that pushed me to really think about listening and why it matters and ultimately to write about it. Since I graduated from university in the late 1990s (with a completely unrelated degree), my work has involved several kinds of writing, research, and media-making. An important early step in this journey was the suggestion from a friend back in 1998 that I do some grassroots journalism for a local independent weekly.[6] Since then, while it has never been my full-time focus and I have gone for long periods without doing any at all, I have repeatedly returned to grassroots journalism, as a writer and as an editor. This kind of work depends, of course, on listening — you listen to what people are saying, you perhaps consult with (listen to) documents, and then you write something that you hope accurately and compellingly synthesizes what you have heard. Over the years, much of what I have done in this area has been about struggles for justice, liberation, and change.

In the early 2000s, in a project that I would come to think of as Talking Radical,[7] I did fifty oral history interviews with long-time activists and organizers from a wide range of movements in cities across Canada. The long subsequent process of working with those generously shared stories was what pushed me to take the step from doing work that made use of listening to thinking critically about what that meant. I constantly returned to questions of what it looked and felt like to listen to, work with, and share material grounded in those stories in a respectful way, a politically appropriate way, an accurate way. I eventually published two books based on fifteen of those interviews.[8]

Not long after the books came out, I started a weekly radio show and podcast called *Talking Radical Radio*, which ran from February 2013 to February 2023.[9] Each of the more than five hundred episodes of the show was organized around an in-depth interview with one or more people involved in some kind of activism or organizing, somewhere in so-called Canada.[10] As the intro to the show put it each week, "We give you the chance to hear many different people who are involved in many different struggles talk about what they're doing, how they're doing it, and why they're doing it, in the belief that such listening can strengthen all of our efforts to change the world." It was broadcast on community radio stations across the country — usually about a dozen at any given point, though how many and which would fluctuate — and was available online in lots of different ways. Again, I spent a lot of time listening at every stage of that work and a lot of time thinking about listening.

Since pretty much the beginning of the show, I was also doing my best to write another book. A project that I had initially imagined as about something very different became, through a series of incremental changes and strategic reboots, this book. The critical moment came when I decided that my latest attempt, which was drawing on material from interviews done for the show, just wasn't working. I realized that I was more interested in writing a book grounded not so much in the content of my interviews but in thinking through the implications of the listening I was doing and the listening being done at every stage of struggle by those I had interviewed.

this book's approach

Though this book is about both listening and movements, it is not primarily about helping the reader become a better listener or a better organizer. Yes, in some places it talks about the doing of such things from the perspective of the individual do-er, but it is not a self-help book or a how-to. I get the appeal of such books, certainly. After all, even granting that none of us has absolute dominion over our own actions, which our culture teaches us to expect and venerate, our actions still often feel like the one piece of our chaotic world over which we can sometimes, partially, imperfectly exert some control. So, it makes sense to want to develop better practices for doing so. But for all that I have been known to read such books myself from time to time, I think that having an entire genre, really an entire industry, devoted to improving *you* with little or no mention of the social world reinforces the exact same neoliberal tendency it flows from — to see everything about the world in terms of individuals.

I think books in this vein that have progressive political intent, that perhaps use language of systemic this or that but that talk mostly about individual actions — a certain subset of books about racism or sexism come to mind, and some books about environmental issues, among others — can be particularly troubling in this regard. Again, they have a range of orientations and can be useful in certain respects, and I have read and benefited from some of them. But at least some take problems that are social, that are fundamentally political, that are about how relations among us are socially organized, and that can only be substantively addressed in collective ways, and teach us to see them as something to be remedied primarily through changes in individual conduct.[11] This kind of framing encourages us to relate to the problems in moral terms, as about individual choices and the goodness or badness of those making them, even if we cloak that in political language. Some of us — I'm thinking particularly about many white people, but it can go along with other socially produced/imposed aspects of self as well — desperately want to be innocent,[12] and ostensibly political books that focus on individual practices for addressing socially produced indignities and harms can peddle the lie that this is in fact possible and downplay the desperate need for collective action.

As I wrote this book, I came to appreciate that it would be easy to treat listening in the same way, as primarily of interest as an individual practice with political relevance. It would be easy to conclude that the appropriate intervention is therefore to improve individual enactment of that practice. This would, in turn, allow readers — meaning privileged readers in particular — to check off boxes related to listening practices, to say, "Yes I do that, therefore I am doing what I can. Therefore I remain a good person." Meanwhile, socially produced indignity and harm in the world would hum along more or less unchanged.

Obviously, this is not saying that we should not strive to figure out how best to move through the world as individuals. Nor is it saying that we shouldn't try to figure out what kinds of listening practices are best suited to our respective contexts. But helping you do that is not what this book is about. This book, rather, is an effort to think through some ideas about the social world, about listening, about knowing, and about change that are inspired and informed by collective struggles for justice and liberation. I also hope that it contributes to such struggles in some small way, though I know that if it does, it will only be indirectly.

I am a firm believer in the value of grappling with ideas of all sorts in ways that are grounded in and relevant to social movements.[13] Some activists and organizers are skeptical of putting time into that kind of work, and I get that. The problems our communities and movements face are immediate and urgent and therefore demand our every effort, leaving few resources for anything else. There is lots of theory out there (and lots of ways of engaging with it) that either are, or at least seem to be, completely irrelevant to ordinary people and our struggles. But ultimately, I do think that it is useful to make collectively re-thinking and re-imagining the world an integral part of our efforts to re-make it. Moreover, while this can and must include writing about ideas that are of direct relevance to tactical and strategic choices, I also think that such re-thinking has value for reaching the futures we want to reach even when it is at an additional remove from the frontlines, so long as it is informed by the frontlines.

So, this book is not going to give you ten easy steps to better listening. It is not going to give you seven amazing social movement hacks. It does not promise you a clear path to personal political purity or even to better movements through listening. What I hope it does offer are ways to think a bit differently about both listening and social movements, and the two of those things together. I hope it pushes you to think about them more complexly and more socially. I hope some of it is a bit uncomfortable, or at least makes you say, "Well what am I supposed to do with *that*?" And if, down the road, after these shifted ways of thinking about listening and movements have simmered and fermented for a good long while, they result in you doing things a little bit differently in some way in your own situation — well, I certainly would not object to that.

This book is divided into three parts. Part 1 is called "What Listening Is," and across its three chapters I explore what we do at the individual level when we listen, then move on to thinking about listening as something that inherently happens between people, and finally to describing a vital, practical role for listening in how our social world as a whole is constituted. Part 2 is called "Listening's Reach and Limits." The first of its two chapters brings together many of the ideas presented in the book to that point and, through examples drawn from my own experience, talks about what listening can tell us about the world. The second is about the down sides of listening — how it fails, how it harms, how it can be bound up with oppressive power, and how there really aren't any easy answers on the individual level to do much about any of that. Part 3 is called "Listening and Change." The first two chapters in this section look at how we resist in everyday ways and at more deliberately collective and self-consciously political modes of struggle, respectively, and talk about what all of that has to do with listening. The final chapter thinks some more about the role that listening plays in how we know the world, and about how we can be more effective in doing that if we listen both to insights about the world derived from collective struggles and to collective struggles and their participants themselves. As important as that can be, though, it still doesn't allow us to escape the limitations described in Part 2, so in the book's Conclusion, I argue that not only is listening central to movements, but movements are the only way we will ultimately be able to create a world that allows listening that is more effective and more just.

I continue to believe that the act of listening to our neighbours, to people across town, and to people around the world is a powerful one. Certainly, listening is not some kind of magical answer, not some kind of universal solvent for the sticky oppressive web that binds us. My epiphany about the power that listening holds was, most definitely, inadequate. But it was not completely wrong, either. As I have already said, some of us listen to some mixture of the circumstances of our own lives and the words of others, and it sparks a deep-down, gut-level urgency that propels us to work for radical change. Listening can bring us the seeds of the knowledge we need to begin working towards that change. Listening is, moreover, the starting point for building the kinds of relationships that are necessary to meaningfully act on that urgency and that knowledge. It would not solve everything on its own, but if more of us listened genuinely and deeply to the everyday experiences of other people and worked hard to match that with relevant theory and action, we would live in a much different world. The time I have spent listening — listening to the people I interviewed for my projects, listening in the context of my own involvement in social movements, and listening in the course of everyday life — has convinced me that this is the case

I hope you will join me as I explore in a bit more detail what listening is, what role it plays in the social world, and, most importantly, how it is at work as we try to understand the world and as we collectively struggle to change it. Thank-you for listening.

part 1

what listening is

chapter one

listening practices

Never, not once, do we get a moment when we are not submerged in the hubbub of the world. From our very beginnings, we are surrounded by a sensory landscape that is vibrant and always in motion, that is noisy and colourful and filled with people. Oh, sure, there is a rhythm to it, a pattern of more and less, high and low. As I type this, I sit in a quiet house on a quiet street, alone but for a cat asleep one floor up, with nothing to hear but the ticking of a clock. I can cast my mind back to moments of even greater quiet, or at least of greater peace. I remember as a kid going for early morning bike rides, setting out from our house on the edge of the little town of Wellesley, speeding along empty country roads with seas of corn on either side, no sound but the crunch of gravel and the rush of the wind, and then stopping for a moment to take in the bright silence. I remember, when I was rather older, a handful of late-night walks through city streets, long after last call, noticing — through the haze of that one final ill-advised beer and through my urgent need to be curled up in bed — the strangeness of still, silent emptiness filling places normally alive with endless motion and noise. And, of course, every night when the clock hits a certain hour, I lie down in a dark room, reduce the stimuli of the world not to zero but as close as I can, and I try to sleep

So, yes, hubbub is a relative term. But even granting that there are some moments that are quieter and dimmer than others, complete silence, complete dark, complete separation from a world in motion is next to impossible. Even if circumstance might somehow put us in solitude and silence that are absolute, we ourselves would carry with us all that we absorbed in moments past. We don't become who we are apart from the endless inputs the world sends our way from our very first awareness, and we always bring all that with us.

This is listening: Constantly, from my first flickers of consciousness, inputs from the world hit me, and I take them in. They change me, at least a little bit. They make me feel something, they allow me to know something, they shape my behaviour, they sediment into who I am. Constantly, I am listening.

Not hearing, but listening

Hearing[1] is based on sound — vibrations travelling through matter. These vibrations, or waves, have a frequency, which we detect as pitch; an intensity, which we experience as loudness; and a timbre, which registers as the qualitative character of the sound. Together, these characteristics provide those of us who can hear with a rich source of information about the world. We detect sound with our ears. The fleshy bits on the outside help to gather the sound waves together and direct them inwards. They travel down a tube, at the end of which they encounter a membrane — our eardrum — and make it vibrate. On the other side lies an air-filled chamber known as the middle ear. It contains three tiny bones, and they vibrate in turn. The final of those three bones is attached to a structure called the oval window, which the vibrations pass through to reach the chambers of a fluid-filled spiral called the cochlea. Inside the cochlea, we have a strip of tissue containing extremely sensitive cells with tiny tufts of hair on them, and when the hair is set in motion by the incoming vibrations, that triggers biochemical responses within the cells. That in turn sets off electrical impulses in the nerve that connects our ears with our brain, which then sorts, processes, and interprets these signals, allowing us (perhaps) to derive information from them. That, crudely and briefly, is hearing.

But this book is not about hearing — it is about listening. My deliberately expansive use of "listening" encompasses not just hearing but all the paths of sense perception through which we encounter and respond to the world. My choice to use this language is in part because "listening" carries with it baggage from its sense-specific origins that does some work I want it to do.

Historian Jonathan Sterne describes a set of binary and contrasting associations with hearing and vision, which have been remarkably stable across many centuries and domains of Western thought — things like "hearing is about affect, vision is about intellect," "hearing places us inside an event, seeing gives us a perspective on the event," and "hearing tends towards subjectivity, vision tends towards objectivity."[2] Hearing and vision have different material bases, of course, and often that is treated as sufficient to explain all of these "hearing is X and vision is Y" associations. Sterne argues, however, that many of these associations have no essential relationship to the biology of how these senses work but are deeply embedded in history and culture. The idea that the practices that comprise our sensory relationships with the world are socially and historically produced is not new, and Sterne quotes a young Karl Marx as writing, "The forming of the five senses is a labor of the entire history of the world down to the present."[3]

It seems to me that particularly when it is *people* who are both sensing and being sensed, dominant understandings and experiences of hearing and vision hint at different kinds of relationships. As a sense that, in dominant understandings, is "concerned with surfaces," "distance," "objectivity," and "intellect,"[4] sight more often falls into a kind of relationship with the rest of the world and particularly with other people that is objectifying and consumptive. I, the one who sees, am active, I have agency, I am fully human. You, the one who is seen, need not do anything to be seen, and it is easy for me to fall into thinking of you as passive, as lacking in agency, as there for me to see or not, and perhaps even not as human as me. Of course this is gendered, to the extent that the ways men so often look at women can be considered a paradigmatic example, but it is also racialized and classed and organized by power in other ways. In contrast, our culture's dominant relationship with hearing makes it just a little bit harder to avoid recognizing that the other person with whom you are in relation in that moment is also active, also has agency, is also fully human, because what you hear is actively created by them. Hearing is, according to Sterne, associated with "interiority," and there is a "connection between sound, subjective self-presence, and intersubjective experience."[5]

Part of the work I want the term "listening" to do, part of the baggage I want to carry with it from its association with hearing, is that "intersubjective" character — its immersion of those who listen in the scenes to which they are listening and into relation with each other. As you will see in the coming chapters, part of why I believe that it is worth thinking and writing about listening is the role it plays in the social world, which is related to this intersubjective character.

On the other hand, it is my hope that using "listening" in a deliberately expansive way and rejecting its presumed exclusive relationship with hearing also helps, in a small way, to denaturalize the relationships between these characteristics and specific senses. I don't actually think that hearing is inherently more intersubjective or less objectifying than vision — those are just dominant cultural assumptions. In addition to the work of scholars like Sterne, who are concerned with historicizing our relationships with our senses, you are perhaps even better off looking to work by writers and scholars in Deaf studies[6] to understand many of these issues, including the fact that sight can just as easily as hearing be a font of the relating between selves that is the basis of the social world. As coming chapters also make clear, hearing, and even listening in the sense that I am using it, are also often consumptive, predatory, and objectifying.

It is certainly possible that using "listening" as I do in this book risks confusion, however explicitly I define it at the start. If what I am trying to do here fails, it risks reinforcing the very sort of naturalized (and often ableist) relationships between hearing and many of the things I talk about in this book that I hope to unsettle. Still, it feels like the best choice available. Language is difficult and sticky, and I will leave it up to you to decide if this choice has been effective or not.

Noticing and attention

Let us imagine ourselves in some moment of the universal hubbub — the heard, seen, felt sensory landscape that always, in one way or another, surrounds us. It might be the squabbling teens, when-does-your-brother-get-here, how-long-should-the-potatoes-go-in-for, turn-that-TV-off, sure-I'll-have-another chaos of a big family dinner. It might be the "Whose streets? Our streets!", catching up with friends, colourful signs, complaining about politics, "Get a job!" yells, and supportive honks of a rally, march, or demo. Or it might even be me, sitting here — a couple of prowling visits from the cat over the course of the afternoon, the irregular passage of cars outside, the text on the screen, and the click and clack of the keyboard at whatever pace I manage to find inspiration.

We never notice everything — we can't. It's patently obvious at a family gathering or demonstration, but doing quiet work in a quiet room really isn't so different. For all that my eyes sweep around when I'm straining to find the right word, the dirty dishes on the coffee table, the cluttered shelves, and the walls hung with family photos and random bits of art don't really register. We are hit with all kinds of inputs from our immediate environment, but we only take in some of them.[7] Before I can do any of the things I need to do to attribute sound waves or light or scent to a particular source or to make meaning from them, I first need to notice them and pay them some attention.

"Noticing" and "paying attention" are not quite the same thing, but they are certainly related — different moments in the same process, maybe, like the initial instant and the enduring middle. Noticing feels instantaneous and involuntary, whereas paying attention has more of the flavour of a deliberate choice about it. I'm not sure that they are as distinct as all that, though. Whether or not we notice something may be decided before we really have a chance to consider it, but (as I discuss later) at least sometimes it still reflects who we are and how the world has shaped us in ways beyond what we control. And, sure, how we direct our attention *can* be something we determine intentionally, but often it isn't. Much of the time, it is swept along in much the same conflicting push and pull of the moment as noticing. Crucially, whether deliberately oriented or not, noticing and paying attention are active processes. We may or may not choose them, but we *do* them, we make them happen through our embodied practices — both those that are detectable externally, like the turning of head or eyes, and those within us that filter and sort and target among the motion and the clamour.

So, what do we notice? What holds our attention? There are probably lots of ways to think about that, but one I find helpful is to look at it through the lens of *proximity*. What is, in all the different ways we can mean that term, close to us? The most obvious dimension to proximity is the physical. We can only notice what is physically near us — a whisper in the next room won't reach our ears and the light bouncing off a smiling face on the other side of town won't reach our eyes. Proximity also plays out in a lot of other ways. Many other factors bring a sound or a sight or a smell closer to our attention or pull it further away. This might be something like volume or suddenness. A heavy book slammed down behind you or an unexpected camera flash are much more insistently close to your attention than a whisper or the generator rumbling outside your window that has receded into your attention's background. It might also be about persistence — if a determined toddler has decided that she is going to tell you what she painted that morning, she is likely going to find a way to make sure you notice, whether or not you think cooking dinner is the higher priority at that moment. Maybe there is something about the character of a sensation that makes it more proximal to your attention and means that you are particularly likely to notice it, when others of similar intensity would be filtered out. As a legacy of a childhood spent immersed in it, I tend to notice the distinctive keen of bagpipes in the air before most other people. Or we might be doing something that draws our attention away from other inputs that hit us — our phone, the conversation we're already in the middle of — or our anxiety might distance us from what is happening around us and make it less likely that we'll notice.

listening practices

There is a persistent myth that portrays what happens next as somehow passive, and us as empty vessels into which experience and meaning are poured. Legendary critical educator Paulo Freire writes of this as the "banking notion of consciousness,"[8] which assumes that "people 'receive' the world as passive entities" and that the act of knowing amounts to a learner "receiving, filing, and storing the deposits"[9] of information provided by teacher, textbook, or world. However, noticing and paying attention are just the first of many active practices that come together under the banner of listening. As Freire's work, not to mention close attention to our own everyday experience, makes clear, we are anything but passive in how we know the world. Knowledge is not something we receive, it is something we make, an active product of our own energies and doings as we take up the inputs resulting from our encounters with the world.

In order to get a sense of the details of these practices, I briefly turn to scholarly models of listening. I have substantial reservations about the extent to which extracting phenomena that we experience at the scale of our everyday lives from their social context and representing them as an idealized process in order to empirically study them can really capture what those phenomena do and mean for us. But I am also a big believer in casting a wide net and in seeing what there is to learn from all sorts of different approaches to knowing the world, so I think they are worth a look. There are plenty of models out there that are either specifically about listening or that incorporate listening as part of modelling some larger process.[10] For the purposes of this book, I am not interested in dissecting different models in a detailed way or in comparing their relative merits and deciding on a particular one to adopt. For one thing, often they treat listening as much more tightly linked to the auditory than I do, though some elements of them are relevant beyond that. What I'm more interested in doing, and what I will do in the rest of this section, is metaphorically stripping these models for parts. I talk in general terms about some of the elements that appear in many different models as a way to get under the surface of listening and tease out the many kinds of doing that comprise it, without getting caught up in either unnecessary detail or in the shortcomings of this approach to studying human activities.

Some models divide the listening practices through which we turn sensory inputs into knowledge into a few distinct levels. We have already talked about the selective character of noticing and attention — we allow certain elements in, we take them up, and we exclude or dismiss the rest. Then we subject those elements to an initial level of processing that some people label "translation." What is it that we are seeing or hearing? Is it a person, a desk, a loaf of bread? If there is language in what we sense, what are the words, what are the symbols, what do they mean? Then the results of that translation are subjected to a different sort of work, a more cognitive and evaluative sort. If translation is the journey from stimulus to basic recognition, this is the process of turning that recognition into meaning and higher-order knowledge.

In some ways, glossing over translation and evaluation as just two elements of the process of listening underestimates the diversity and complexity of what they involve. Even just at the recognition stage, that work is astoundingly complex — things like being able to parse out objects from what would otherwise just register as a field of colours, being able to identify a melody, being able to assign meaning to hand gestures, usually in ways that are so organic, so seamless, that we don't even recognize all of this as something that we are actively doing. If anything, it is even more true for the more evaluative elements of the process. In a broad sense, I think a lot of this stage involves putting whatever knowledge we are producing through our listening in a given moment into relation with our existing knowledge. If you are hearing a friend talk about the party they went to last night, or you are reading a novel, or you are watching a sporting event, you are making something more than the sum of the inputs you received, through a whole set of practices figuring out what you are hearing and seeing means contextually, what you feel about it, what you think about it, what matters about it, how it reflects on the people involved, how it connects to other parties/novels/games or to other things more tangentially related — all of it. Even if someone is trying to convince you of some set of (supposed) facts, evaluating what they tell you is usually not as simple as assigning it a clear "true" or "false." You assess how reliable your new knowledge is, whether and how it is significant, what it points to beyond itself. Does it fit well with what you already know? If not, what then? Do you just accept the inconsistency, dismiss the new, transform the old? Your feelings play into all of this, too, as much as some would deny it, as well as your attachment to things like your sense of self and your instincts about how the world *should* work, never mind how it does. Putting new listening into relation with existing knowledge produces frictions, consonances, dissonances, harmonies, resonances — it becomes, itself, a whole new source of meaning and knowledge. Moreover, as we do all of this, we are producing not just new knowledge in a narrow sense but a complex weave of stories, feelings, and imagination.

We enact all these practices, and countless more, across a whole range of deliberateness and rigour, perhaps carefully considering each aspect, but more often deploying split-second, gut-level, short-hand judgement. In practice, most of the time, this happens smoothly and quickly and without much thought. You might think of it as having a repertoire of short-hand practices for navigating the perpetual chaos of the world without being overwhelmed by it. Some people use the language of "schemas" and "scripts" to convey the idea that we often work from pre-existing templates and routines to be able to quickly categorize, assess, store, and respond to encounters and the knowledge that we make from them.

Another set of practices that are integral to many of the kinds of processing we do as part of listening are related to memory. Scientific models generally understand there to be two different kinds of memory — short-term or working memory and long-term memory. The former is about storing knowledge as we process it and the latter is more about storing for future recall, and the practices that we engage in to produce, evaluate, and otherwise process knowledge involve making sophisticated and varied use of both. One important outcome of evaluating new inputs involves decisions (again, active but often not conscious) about what ends up being stored in long-term memory.

And a final and extremely diverse set of practices that at least sometimes fall under the banner of "listening" in the sense I am using it are externally oriented responses to a given moment of encounter — we noticed, paid attention, translated, processed, and stored, and then as an extension of that same process, we take some action in response. The pan is hot, so we pull our hand back, or the recipe calls for a cup of flour, so we get the bag out of the cupboard and add it. As we act, we direct our attention in the next moment to the cold of the water running over our hand, to stirring the contents of the mixing bowl, or to something else entirely. It may not always make sense to include these subsequent actions in how we think about listening, but to capture the sense of responsiveness to the world that is important to how I am using the term, I leave open the possibility that at least sometimes these externally focused responses are integral to the listening process.

When you take a peek under the hood like this, "listening" opens up as a highly variable cluster of things we do related to sense perception, attention, cognition, evaluation, memory, sociality, and more. What practices we employ, how we combine them, and how much effort we put into them vary a great deal depending on the context and on what we are trying to achieve.[11]

listening is learned

Most of us are born with some complement of biological infrastructure to take in sensory inputs — the specifics can vary from person to person, but most of us have some.[12] However, much of the doing through which that infrastructure is deployed in the service of listening is something we have to learn. You are not born understanding language or being able to identify a shark or a footstool or a deck of cards. You do not automatically know how to turn the bloviations of an angry white man into a commitment to grassroots organizing in opposition to his agenda, or how to go from a series of lines and colours on a screen to bleak absurdist humour about the state of the world. Some forms of responsiveness may be innate, like revulsion at obviously putrid food, but even then, it is all too easy to fail to turn a not-quite-right scent into a decision not to eat something — at least sometimes, that too must be learned.

And how do we learn? Through our listening — through taking in, taking up, and making meaning from the words and world around us. This is obvious when it comes to knowledge you might describe as propositional[13] — meaning, knowledge that we can put into words, like the capital of France, the labour theory of value, or the average blood pressure of a healthy adult. If we know such things, it is because we heard or saw them. But it is just as true when it comes to learning embodied practices, like how to shoot a basketball or play the piano. A mixture of watching other people play, spending hours messing around with a ball and a hoop, and getting pointers from a coach will, together, help you develop your skills. All those things, including the long grind of practice, involve various kinds of taking in and taking up of sensory input — not just words, but how doing it this way or that feels in your body. This, too, is listening. The obvious implication, here, is that since we need to learn how to listen, and learning happens *through* listening, then our listening in one moment must be shaped by our listening in earlier moments. We learn to listen by listening.

As described above, listening involves both enacting a range of non-propositional practices and, as we derive and asses meaning from what we have taken up, making use of our existing store of propositional knowledge. All these things have to be learned. It is intuitively clear that the existing propositional knowledge that we deploy as we listen came from past listening. But the learned character of the practices that comprise listening is not always so obvious. Take noticing and paying attention. It is easy to think of those as automatic responses to stimuli. But, again, the lens of proximity can be helpful in teasing out the different things that feed into them. Some elements of proximity are more about the stimulus in question, like its loudness, brightness, or physical closeness, but there are others that are social, and those are learned. Take, for example, two of the many gut-level factors that feed into our noticing and attention, *out-of-placeness* and *aboutness*.

"Out-of-placeness" points to our assessment of the relationship of something that we encounter to the context in which it is happening. If something that bumps into our senses feels like it does not belong, then we reflexively treat it as more proximal and we are more likely to notice it and give it our attention than if it is expected, consistent with context, fully belonging. For instance, our home and our neighbourhood probably have a particular profile of typical night-time noises, and living there and hearing those noises have shaped our gut-level expectations of what we might hear while lying in bed at night. If we live in an old farmhouse far out in the country, we learn to expect a different normal and to mark different sounds as out of place than if we live in the downtown of a major city. That gets inside of us in a visceral way, informing not just our intellectualized understanding of the world around us but what wakes us up, what freaks us out.

"Aboutness" has to do with the relationship between what is being noticed and the person doing the noticing. If, in my snap, in-the-moment judgement, something I encounter as I move through the world is about me, I am more likely to notice it and give it my attention. This is why you are more likely to pick out your own name than a random phrase from a conversation happening on the other side of a noisy room. Or take the nightmare factory that is social media — my rapid, casual scrolling involves ongoing, near-instantaneous assessment of what is flitting past, including for its aboutness. A given chunk of content is more likely to pull my notice and attention when it is about a place I have lived, a pop culture franchise I enjoy, a struggle that has touched my life, or something else I have, through my past listening, determined to be in some sense about me. Again, while this can be a conscious and cognitive determination, it often feels much more in-the-body and instinctive. But, even so, it is learned.

Practices comprising all the other elements of listening are learned as well. This is true even when we think about practices of sense perception. The details of how exactly biological change and learning interweave as the visual sense develops in infants don't matter for our purposes, but I feel confident in asserting that it is not just a matter of passive changes in the infrastructure for doing but at least some element of learning how to do. Or we can turn back to Jonathan Sterne's work, where he documents the historical emergence of new bodily practices used to listen in the context of early sound reproduction technologies — people had to learn how to do those things.[14] Or think about learning a second language. Depending on the language you are trying to learn, you may have to train yourself to make distinctions among sounds that your first language does not require. English, for example, does not use differences in tone to distinguish between words that otherwise sound the same, so if you are learning a language that does, such as Mandarin, you have to develop new listening practices to be able to identify those differences.

All the higher-level scripts and schemas through which we make and assess and decide what to do with knowledge are built from past learning as well. That is how a skilled chef has become able to turn the sounds and sights and smells in their kitchen into meaning, judgement, and action. It is how any of us have developed our own ways of extracting and assessing meaning from a video essay or a book of nonfiction. None of which is to say anything about how effective these practices might be in a given instance or how well they would hold up to scrutiny. But they are, nonetheless, a product of all our prior listening.

listening brings the social world inside of you

So, you listen to the world, take it in, take it up, and make meaning from it. That meaning, that knowledge, that learning shapes who you are, what you are able to do, and how you subsequently move through the world. As part of that, it shapes your future listening. Think about that for a minute: You listen to the world. You take it in. It shapes how you listen in the future. The implication here is that your listening is moulded by your experience of the world. If you had different experiences, you would have listened to different things, made different knowledge, and learned different practices — including different listening practices.

Take an obvious example: imagine an ancestor of mine. It seems likely that, six hundred years ago, some of my ancestors were peasants in the Scottish Lowlands. There is no doubt that a person making their way in the world through agricultural labour in rural Ayrshire in the 1420s developed a different set of listening practices than me. Our worlds are very different, and therefore so are our sensory landscapes; in a context that is industrialized, mechanized, and computerized, my survival depends on different sensory practices than my ancestor's did. Think, too, about the practices that are about the translation, evaluation, and processing through which we make knowledge from what we hear and see. There are drastic differences between the rural pre-Reformation Catholic frameworks of meaning that would have enveloped and shaped how my ancestor did such things and the forms of meaning prevalent in early twenty-first-century urban Canada and the secular left bent of my specific trajectory. How could we *not* have different practices for turning our sense perception into knowledge, stories, feelings, and imagination?

It might be tempting to take all the possible differences in listening practices between my hypothetical ancestor and me and place them in a singular category called "culture." It is certainly reasonable to understand at least some of the norms in each social context around who or what we listen to, and how and when we do that listening, as in part related to culture. As well, some of the listening practices related to making meaning about the world — our scripts and schemas, the store of knowledge we accumulate over our lives — can also be understood as having been shaped by our culture. This is not just relevant to comparing myself with my ancestor. For instance, I can think back to moments in my involvement in grassroots solidarity work with Indigenous Peoples and Indigenous struggles which starkly illustrated differences in cultural norms between them and white Canadians related to practices for listening and knowing. Of course, both of those groups are themselves culturally diverse, which is no doubt reflected in the breadth of listening practices within each. In any case, as important a factor as culture can be, it is worth being cautious about how we use it as an explanation. As the extensive anti-racist critiques of Canadian state multiculturalism make clear,[15] "culture" very easily gets used as a catch-all category to explain difference, in ways that obscure the workings of power and the social organization of a given situation, to the benefit of those groups that are already powerful.

It would be possible, I suppose, to speculate in much greater detail about the ways in which this ancestor and myself might have different listening practices due to the differences in our environment and experiences. But in the context of this book I am more interested in taking up questions related to power and exploring what it means for those of us in the twenty-first century to develop our listening practices in the context of a social world shaped by oppression, injustice, and resistance. Our social world is riven by and organized into white supremacy, settler colonialism, patriarchy, ableism, heterosexism, cissexism, capitalism, and many other axes of power. They are very much a part of the social world that gets inside of us, including shaping the listening practices through which we know and become able to intervene in the world.

There is an element of this that is broad and overarching. One consequence of living in a world with oppressive power organized along these axes is that it, in practical and material ways, influences what happens in our everyday lives, what we encounter, what reaches our senses. That is, it shapes the raw material for our listening and learning, which in turn shapes our subsequent listening. As part of that, we listen to all manner of stories, ideas, and images that are, explicitly or implicitly, telling us about the world. Any social order tends to have a range of dominant stories, ideas, and images — a common sense through which the way things are is portrayed as being right and stable and the way things should be. Italian Marxist Antonio Gramsci talked about this in his notion of hegemony, where he sought to understand how the ruling class maintains power not only through overt coercion but also through the consent of those ruled.[16] A lot can be debated about how exactly that works, and I argue for a more multidimensional understanding of power than pre-Second World War European revolutionaries generally held, but the relevant point is that we have no choice but to listen to these stories, ideas, and images. They are usually not in the form of crude, obvious propaganda, but rather are those assumptions that weave quietly through the background of seemingly different elements of culture. They are not monolithic and are not the only ideas out there for us to listen to. But they are everywhere, and we cannot avoid them. Our prior listening to these dominant common-sense ideas is inevitably part of what shapes our practices as we assess the new knowledge that we produce through listening. They weave through our scripts and schemas and other practices and through the pool of existing knowledge that is our reference point for assessing the new.

In thinking about how our listening is shaped by our experiences of the world, however, we also need to keep in mind the active character of that listening. We cannot avoid listening to the dominant stories and ideas that surround us and that inevitably shape us, but what exactly that looks like is far from predetermined. As the late anarchist anthropologist David Graeber and archaeologist David Wengrow note in their far-ranging look at humanity's earlier millennia, *The Dawn of Everything*, "skeptics and non-conformists exist in every human society"[17] and not just in those we stereotype as "modern" or "free." There are inevitably eccentrics, weirdos, and dissidents who reject dominant understandings and dominant practices, who scoff at ideologies or cosmologies or other frameworks that their neighbours adhere to, who evaluate the inputs from other people and the world differently than most around them, who make different choices as a result. Their point is larger than this, but what matters for our discussion here is how it applies to our practices of listening and knowing and to the base of knowledge that we build over time. Because all of that is active, a given set of starting conditions and a given environment can still lead to people who do things in lots of different ways. This is path dependent. Each step you take in a new direction incrementally changes what you are exposed to, what knowledge you have, and the listening practices in your repertoire, so the ways in which you engaged with your sensory inputs in a previous decade might look very different than how you do so now.[18]

Perhaps even more important, while we all live in the same world, our experiences of said world are vastly different, precisely because of how our communities, our lives, and the world are organized along those axes of power. You and I and those people over there might have been born within territory claimed by so-called Canada, but our lives are not the same. The specific character of our local environments, the specific stories we have encountered, and the details of the sensory flow that has washed over us have been different, to a greater or lesser extent. In particular, the mix of harm and benefit we experience from those axes of power is different.

We will explore this in greater detail later, but this means, among other things, that we develop different listening practices, as one element of selves oriented in different ways with respect to the current state of the world. One way of naming how our knowledge of the world is shaped by who we are and where we know the world from is "standpoint." Crucial writing about this idea has come from a range of feminist theorists and writers focused on race and white supremacy.[19] For me, though writers in this tradition don't always use the language of standpoint or focus on epistemology per se, thinking about the relevance of how we are socially situated to what we experience, to how we know the world, and to how we must act politically has most crucially been shaped by reading the work of Black feminists as well as other anti-racist feminists.[20] Though I do not stick to any individual model of standpoint, much of what I have to say about listening is broadly influenced by these interrelated traditions.

In all these ways, as we learn to listen by listening, we are shaped by the fact that our sensory landscape is socially organized along multiple axes of unjust power, oppression, and resistance. For all that our journeys through the hubbub are active and complex and not some caricatured determinism, the specifics of our experiences of that landscape — particularly our experiences of benefit and harm — matter deeply to what we listen to, to how and what we learn, and to the listening practices we develop.

chapter two

listening to each other

While listening may be a diverse and complicated set of practices enacted by each of us as individuals, it is more than that too. When the hubbub surrounds us, when its many forms and frequencies bump into our senses, it is often the sights and sounds of life, and particularly of *each other,* that stand out. Much of the time, it is voices and bodies, images and words — that is, people and our emanations — that feel most like they matter, that feel more proximal, more worthy of the limited resource that is our attention. For many of us, listening to other people saturates our lives and our consciousness.[1] Yet the implications of this reality for how we think about listening are rarely appreciated.

what we say about listening

As a culture, we have a lot to say about the listening that happens (or doesn't) between people, often in the form of advice about doing it more or better. As one book puts it, "Advice about listening is white noise. It's so common and so boring we no longer even hear it."[2] Sometimes, we talk about it in ways that explicitly foreground listening, but often we bring it into discussions framed around other things, sometimes without even using the word "listening." It appears in one way or another in books about parenting, presentation skills, having good conversations, leadership, relationships, sexuality, and lots of other things.[3] Listening also regularly appears in at least implicit ways in books related to social movements and other collective efforts striving for justice and liberation.

In some popular sources about listening, the admonition to do so is not necessarily accompanied by instructions on how — it presumes we know how to do it, and we just need to be told where and when. It is framed as a suggestion that here, in this instance, to these people, for this purpose, you must listen. Take communication skills coach and media strategist Jim Gray's book *How Leaders Speak*,[4] which is oriented towards a business audience. He does not articulate it explicitly in terms of listening, but a lot of his advice for how to make a good impression with your next big presentation has to do with being attentive to your audience as you prepare and as you speak. Who are they? What do they need and want? What are they expecting from you? All of those are about listening in the expansive sense that I am talking about it.

Many other sources, however, do include advice about how to listen better. A book about parenting teens offers a very common piece of listening advice — the idea of "saying exactly what the other person has just said to you" in the course of conversation, to make them "feel that you heard them and that you are fully sharing their experience."[5] Author Loni Coombs, writing on the website of prolific mainstream advice-giver Dr. Phil, includes in her "Six Tips for Effective Listening" facing the person who is speaking and maintaining eye contact, focusing on what they are saying, and trying not to get defensive.[6] Dr. Phil's own advice on such matters includes, yes, the idea of mirroring what the other person says and also regularly checking in with them to make sure you are understanding, choosing an environment conducive to conversation, and actively evaluating your own filters that might be getting in the way of understanding what they are saying.[7] In the book *How to Talk to Anyone,* which in its subtitle makes the clickbait-y promise of providing *92 Little Tricks for Big Success in Relationships,* you find the advice about mirroring yet again, along with other insights like matching the other person's mood and tone, "listen[ing] to your conversation partner's every word for clues about his or her preferred topic," and being extravagantly solicitous when on the phone and you hear some background noise by asking if they might need to attend to whatever you have heard — "Whether she does or not, she'll know you're a top communicator for asking."[8] Often, when listening is addressed in books that focus on something else, or in shorter pieces in the popular media, the advice is these sorts of short, practical, almost technical suggestions for how to conduct yourself in the moment of encounter — some of which are reasonably useful, as far as they go, though they also range to the patently obvious and in a different direction to the faintly absurd.

There are also many books that treat listening with greater depth and sophistication. Such books approach the subject from a wide range of perspectives and, like the sources above, vary in terms of whether listening is present as an explicit focus or an implicit grounding.[9] Rather than listening, they might centre conversation or practices of connecting with other people. They might treat listening as valuable in itself or perhaps as an approach to building a more just society.[10] They might talk about listening from a Buddhist perspective,[11] a Christian one,[12] or a scholarly one based on the latest empirical research.[13] You can easily find how-to manuals pitched at business leaders[14] and evidence-based practical advice aimed at listening better in order to improve familial and intimate relationships.[15] Such books approach listening in thoughtful ways, in moralistic ways, in instrumental ways, in analytical ways.

Perhaps not surprisingly, many of these books put a great deal of energy into giving individuals advice about how to listen better. In some, we are told that we can improve our listening through slowing down, cultivating curiosity about one another, and working to be open to being disturbed and having our preconceptions challenged. In some, we are encouraged to combine relaxation, focus, and a desire to learn into an ongoing discipline-like practice. We may be advised of the power of empathy, pauses, or carefully curated questions. We are instructed to develop our listening through mindfulness and the deliberate release of distraction and judgement and told that our listening will be improved by putting ourselves imaginatively in the shoes of others. There are suggestions across these different sources for managing our emotions in order to listen more effectively, recognizing the ways that our existing filters and our own needs interfere with our listening, and allowing ourselves to be vulnerable. Some of these books even warn against the kinds of technical fixes for listening that fill briefer sources, sometimes while offering advice that doesn't sound so very different. Despite the breadth of approaches and the much greater depth of attention in these books than in those sources cited earlier, they often end up covering similar ground.

listening is more than an individual act

The similarities found among these seemingly diverse sources extend beyond the overlap in the practical advice they give. They also share some underlying assumptions about the nature of listening, one of which I discuss here and another of which I take up later in the book.

Most mainstream, popular sources frame listening as adhering, in one way or another, to individuals, though the details vary. For some, it is a choice, something this person chooses to do but that person does not. For some, it is a skill that individuals possess, a result of technical know-how that can be identified and shared. For others, it is a capacity or trait — something that we can do not only because of having the right kind of knowledge but because of being the right kind of self. Still others frame it more as a practice, a discipline along the lines of meditation. There are other framings as well, and some approaches combine them. But across this variation, listening is treated at its heart as a product of what *I* have, *I* choose, *I* am, or *I* do.

It's not just books and articles — it's also how most of us understand listening, most of the time. After all, "listening" for many of us defaults to "that thing I do with my ears." We disposed of the presumed inherent relationship to hearing earlier, but even when we account for that and expand our definition to something like "those things I do to take in, take up, and make meaning from the world," practices enacted by individuals are still mostly what we centre in our everyday usage of the word.

And this is, certainly, one important aspect of listening. When you are paying attention to a lecture or a podcast, or when you listen compassionately as I pour my heart out, it is *you* who are listening. When a counsellor and student work to help the latter develop better practices for focusing in class, or when an executive follows the advice in an article about leadership and solicits input from subordinates, the suggested changes are clearly enacted by individual people. But as intuitive as it might seem, things are not quite that simple. In fact, it is obvious that at least some aspects of listening cannot just be about the individual. We cannot, logically, listen to other people — their voices or whatever other traces they leave in the world — without other people. For me to listen, you must speak. For you to read, I must have written.

how voices reach us

Think about the practical ways in which listening to other people, their voices, and whatever else they do that our selves can detect weave through our lives. Given my particular embodied experience, the most basic way in which voices reach me is through the spoken words of the people immediately around me. My partner tells me about her day. My son goes on at great length about his current video game obsession. My mother makes sure I have the latest news from relatives across the sea. A friend asks for advice regarding a woman he knows full well he shouldn't be crushing on but is. A dear friend, for the nth time, talks about the impossible work/life bind that holds her captive. Someone I have just met tells me about his tech sector job and opines about how Canadian weather "has no chill" compared to back home in Northern Ireland. Someone I haven't seen in ages shares gossip about people we both know.

To a greater or lesser extent, we are also listening not only to our interlocutor but to the context in which locution takes place — we hear "You're fired!" differently when it is being said in deadly earnest by our boss than when it is a frustrated four-year-old with hands on hips. As I explore more in a future chapter, often voices carry with them more than just the surface content of words. In other situations, embodied presence is all there is — no communication is intended, and I am listening in the absence of voice, however broadly understood. It is the tread across the floor upstairs. It is the flow of other cars around you on the highway. Sometimes, your embodied presence communicates when you are unaware or even when you would rather it did not, as when you attempt to mask your exhaustion or distress, yet they bleed through anyway.

In this era, many of the voices we listen to and many of the encounters we have are not directly with embodied human beings at all. Technology brings voices and a wealth of other communicative forms to us, however close or far we may be from other humans in "meatspace." For much of each day, I face either screen or page, both of which work the magic of transporting the voices of the absent into my brain. Screens in particular, at least when they are connected to social media, are a cross between a highway and a funnel. Sometimes, they are exactly the high speed, high efficiency information conveyance that we need; sometimes, they extend our capacity to listen to voices we would never encounter in other ways;

but sometimes, it feels like what is rushing through will drown us, and it draws us into practices and relations that are deeply troubling.[16]

Yet even in the absence of your phone, your family, or the latest novel, still your experience and your consciousness are saturated with voices. Due both to temperament and vocation, I spend significant chunks of my days with no other people around. Screens and pages fill some of that, but far from all. Yet even then, voices surround me. For one thing, I talk to myself a lot. Beyond being a mildly peculiar habit I do my best not to indulge when other people might hear, I think it is also an extension into sound of a way of relating to ourselves and the world that is, if not necessarily universal, at least common. Certainly not all of us actually vocalize, but I think many of us engage in some form of communicative exchange across internal difference. For me, it is often about trying to reach clarity about whatever it is I am thinking about in that moment, perhaps as part of making a decision, forming an opinion, or navigating commitments, pressures, or desires that are pulling in different directions. We also talk about listening to the less deliberate emanations of our selves — listening to our bodies when we are tired or hungry or listening to our emotions as we try to communicate better with a partner.

It is not just our own voices that we engage with internally. Memory allows us to listen to the voices of others when no one else is around, whether that is replaying in painful detail some mortifying interaction we had earlier that day or whether it is recalling the overall gist of input we received from the other members of our grassroots collective about what to put in the flyer we're designing. It also happens in a more imaginative mode. Based on prior listening, we construct, in our minds, models of the people in our lives, and use those models to project what they *would* say about a given topic or situation. It is quite common, I think, to hear internally the echoes of parental disapproval at something we have just done when no parent is around, or to hear the laugh of a partner at a joke she would love even when she's in another city.

how voices matter

Think about the practical ways in which what I have just described matters to our experience of living. Listening to each other is central to the formation of both *I* and *we*. We saw in the last chapter that our selves are shaped through our journey of listening to the sensory landscape that surrounds us. I framed it that way to make it as expansive and inclusive as possible, but of course a big part of that is not about the world in general but about listening specifically to other people. We never exist independently of the people around us. *I* forms as part of *we*, from the very start and throughout our lives. So, listening to other people matters in part because it is so central to what makes us who we are.

In a deeply related way, listening is also central to our relationships. Whatever intensity or scope, whatever context or purpose, there is no *we* without listening. Depth of intimacy, strength of trust, and shared life cannot in any meaningful way happen without listening to each other's voices. There are many more people with whom we may never be close, with whom intimacy is not a goal, but with whom getting along, understanding each other a little bit, and collaborating in the moment to solve whatever lies before us will undoubtedly smooth our passage through the world.

Listening to voices and taking in through eyes and ears the various and sundry communications of others is also central to how we know the world. It is, in fact, the only way we can know beyond the confines of our own local environments, understood both in physical and social terms. I can move about, of course, but even so, most of the world will never be nearby. The only way that I, personally, will know anything about the Amazon rainforest or even that it exists at all is if I encounter words and images from other people that tell me about it. Even for things that are physically close, that mere fact will allow me to know certain things but not others. From the vagaries of the social assistance system to the spectrum of possibilities for moving through the world as Black, Indigenous, or trans, or as a wheelchair user, to the true magnitude of Canadian state violence, what little I know is from listening to friends, to organizers I interview, to books I read, and so on. Beyond just knowledge narrowly conceived, we are taking in stories, feelings, and imagination from others, which in turn are informing us, shaping us, and moving us into closer relation with others (or not).

Bound together with all of this is our capacity to act — much of our doing depends on listening to each other. We collaborate, we coordinate, we plan, we decide. Whether it is the ordering of the most hierarchical and rigid workplace, the informal with-ness of friends on a vacation, or the urgent assessment and adjustment as a direct action goes catastrophically not to plan, we cannot act in the world except in the most isolated of ways without the kind of ongoing, reciprocal exchange enabled by listening.

Listening to people is also central to many of the pleasures that come from listening, whether that takes the form of the delights of music, our continuous reinvention of the species-old pastime of telling stories, or the wonderful intimacy of hearing others talk about their own lives.

listening and making change

Given how central listening to each other is to *we*, to knowing, and to doing in general, it should be no surprise that this is also true of our collective efforts to change the world for the better. We examine the interrelation of listening and social movements in more detail later in the book but consider for a moment the visions for change — rich, far-reaching, and diverse — to be found in the words of many differently situated organizers, activists, revolutionaries, and radical thinkers. If you slice through what they say, you will find perhaps mentions of and inevitably pointers towards listening in their imaginings of future worlds, in the *we* they think is necessary to get there, and in their understandings of how change happens. They might not use the language of "listening" directly, but if you pay close attention, the presumption of it is not just present but pervasive.

The work of many radical Indigenous writers who envision paths towards liberatory Indigenous futures — and I'm thinking specifically of Leanne Betasamosake Simpson and Pamela Palmater, but it is true of many others — talks in part about the relations called for in both those futures and the struggles to reach them. Certainly, the work of building "relationships based on deep reciprocity, respect, noninterference, self-determination, and freedom"[17] or ways of work grounded in "patience, listening, and understanding multiple perspectives by hearing from all voices who want to be heard"[18] clearly and centrally require listening. Those seem to be elements of larger visions that prioritize a deep and profound practice of responsiveness in life and in struggle that is consistent with my use of the word "listening," even as it exceeds it.

Or you can look to the writing of mid-twentieth-century Guinean anti-colonial revolutionary Amilcar Cabral.[19] This is perhaps the most broadly circulated quote from his work: "Hide nothing from the masses of our people. Tell no lies. Expose lies whenever they are told. Mask no difficulties, mistakes, failures. Claim no easy victories." In its exhortation to a revolutionary honesty, it is premised not only on communication by those at the centre of the struggle but on the broader colonized population taking in, taking up, and acting on those words as they move along the fraught path towards liberation. He also calls for a commitment to constant listening on the part of revolutionaries themselves: "Learn from life, learn from our people, learn from books, learn from the experiences of others. Never stop learning." In multiple senses and multiple directions, listening is, for Cabral, a key part of the *how* of change.

Migrant justice organizer Harsha Walia writes of the role of non-Indigenous people in struggles for decolonization, recognizing that "support" and even "solidarity" are not enough, but rather that a deeper and more sophisticated approach to being in relation is called for and that such work "requires us to challenge a dehumanizing social organization that perpetuates our isolation from each other and normalizes a lack of responsibility to one another and the Earth."[20] Whatever else that involves, it sounds like greater listening to each other and to the world is one element. Prominent Canadian feminist Judy Rebick speaks of how central learning to listen to other women has been to her experience of feminism.[21] Radical Montreal-based musician Norman Nawrocki passionately argues for activists and organizers to do more to integrate music and the arts into their work, in part because of their capacity to catalyze listening in new and different ways.[22] Famous community organizer Saul Alinsky warns of how important it is not just to talk at the people you are trying to organize, but to listen to them long and well.[23] Abolitionist organizers Mariame Kaba and Kelly Hayes emphasize the centrality of listening in movement building: "It is our ability to constructively engage with other people that will ultimately power our efforts. ... And that skill of constructive engagement starts with listening."[24] Long-time revolutionary anti-fascist Michael Novick,[25] activists and writers Leah Hunt-Hendrix and Astra Taylor,[26] Marxist intellectual Vijay Prashad,[27] US-based radical adrienne maree brown,[28] and many, many others also identify a role for listening in their respective political visions.

An entire book could be written tracing a genealogy of shifting practices and modes of listening across different movements, eras, and struggles for change, and different radical thinkers, though I will leave that project for someone else. I suspect as well that many political critiques among and across the diverse movements and traditions touched on above could be reframed as arguments about how, when, and to whom listening should be happening. But, nonetheless, for all of them, listening plays a role — and much of that is the listening we do to each other.

listening requires other people

The popular sources surveyed earlier in the chapter don't exactly deny the reality that other people are central to our listening. In fact, some of them talk at great length about the value of listening in the context of our relationships with other people. One source that takes up listening on the basis of psychological research goes so far as to say, "While it's possible in the abstract to separate speakers and listeners, in practice they are inextricably intertwined. Listening is codetermined."[29] This important observation teeters on the edge of diving into examining listening in ways that go beyond the individual, but the book avoids taking the plunge, and most of the other sources above do not even go that far. For the most part, while they recognize the value of listening in the context of our relationships, it is still conceptualized pretty much exclusively as something done by the individuals in those relationships.

But all those ways that listening to others weaves through our lives, and all the practical ways it matters, point to the need to go beyond that. Listening is certainly our individual practices, but it is more too. It is reciprocal and collaborative and premised on our ubiquitous relation with others — those things are not peripheral but central. As we have seen, the very shapes of ourselves, our existence in relation, our knowing and acting in the world, all depend — completely and utterly, in all these ways and many more — on listening that presumes ongoing, continuous, dynamic exchange with others. This *withness* is not incidental to listening but integral to what it is and what it does in our lives, inherent and internal to listening as it actually happens. It is always about something happening between us, something emerging, something relational, in ways that listening conceptualized primarily as individual choice or practice fails to capture.

In the coming chapters, I take seriously the idea that listening has meaning and importance beyond that individual level and explore the broader significance of its role in how we exist in relation with each other. At least for a while, I refuse separateness and figure out what it really means that speakers and listeners are so inextricably intertwined.

chapter three

listening weaves the world

Hubbub, I said in the first chapter.
Each other, I said in the second.

From the beginning, we take shape together, not apart. We do not proceed as solitary souls and then only at some later point bump into others. Rather, we are surrounded by and interrelated with them from the very start. The churning sensory landscape is never absent from our eyes and ears, and voices are always the sea in which we swim. No one, to paraphrase John Donne,[1] is an island and all of us are part of a bigger whole, and Alfred, Lord Tennyson once observed, "I am a part of all that I have met."[2] All of us, from our first moments, are always already *social*.

In order to explore what that means and what it has to do with our sensory landscape, with voices, and with listening, an obvious next step would be for me to lay out my own understanding of the social world. I would talk about capitalism and settler colonialism, white supremacy and ableism, and all the rest. I would talk about institutions and states, injustice and collective struggle. But I want to take a different approach in this book — not because I think those things don't matter; they are central to my understanding of the world and to how I continue to talk about it throughout this book. But they are also things you can learn about in lots of other sources.

Instead, I approach talking about the social world in a way that is at least partially informed by this book's focus — listening. I dig into our experiences of trying to understand the world as people who are *in* the world and who can only do so through situated, embodied listening.

As I discuss in greater detail below, part of this means recognizing that we might encounter many different accounts of the social world. By "accounts of the social world," I mean analyses, theories, stories, or modes of thought that help us make sense of and name our experiences and those of others. They help us to make predictions about what goes on around us and to understand how the world beyond our own experience works. Such accounts can be better or worse, both in general and in specific contexts. But even the best of them are inevitably partial and incomplete. Yes, there is a world out there for us to know, and we *can* know it, but we can't know it perfectly or completely, and the work of trying to know it from our place in the middle of it is inevitably ... well, a bit of a muddle. So rather than do the same as so many other books and offer you yet another supposedly singular and complete account of the social world, this chapter explores that muddle from our place in the middle of it, from our own imperfect mix of existing practices for listening and knowing. It aims not to replace those practices but instead offers a few possible tools to augment them. By the end, I wind back to a more explicit consideration of what all this has to do with listening.

our experience

I start thinking about the social world from the vantage of our experience of it. I do this because I think we are kidding ourselves when we pretend there is any other place to start. I do it because it flows so obviously from how this book understands listening. And I do it because I think it is a useful, even powerful, approach.

I am not making naive claims about experience giving us some kind of transcendent access to truth. Our experience and our ability to turn it into knowledge, meaning, and narrative are shaped by the material, linguistic, and other ideological seas in which we swim. Appealing to experience, or at least how I am suggesting that we do so, is not an attempt to escape all of that but to engage with it. That engagement must be critical and attentive to how our capacities to listen to, make meaning from, and respond to our experience are socially produced and are not some direct and unvarnished reflection of reality. Nor am I suggesting that we should valorize our own experience over everyone else's — this is not an argument for saying "X happened to me and Y happened to you, therefore X is true" but rather "I experienced X and you experienced Y; how are they both part of some larger social reality?"

Prioritizing experience as a starting point for understanding the world is important precisely because experience is the stuff of our lives. It is an ethical and political stance to say that our pain matters, our pleasure matters, our suffering matters, our thriving matters — to know what is just and what is not, what is good and what is bad, because of the impacts on the texture of the everyday lives of me, you, her, them, all of us. It is a small step from there to adopting an approach to knowing the world with that value at the centre. Our reference point, our grounding, that to which we must constantly return is the ordinary moments in our ordinary lives. Those moments are how we assess value and relevance. Those moments are the source of our questions. Those moments are how we test the answers we arrive at. Of course, as we do that, we do not exempt those moments from our scrutiny — we question how they came to be and try to understand how the world binds us in messy complexity such that our everyday experience is not innocent but implicated. It is not a clear window into the world but a perpetually cloudy one, not a way to jump to the pure and the certain but a way to begin to wrestle with the partial and the unreliable. But, nonetheless, we begin from experience, we return there, we centre what we find there.

There are lots of ways we could talk about how we experience the world, but I want to keep it simple: We are *selves* who are constantly *encountering* people and things, and as we do so we are *listening*. Barring some psychedelic, spiritual, or psychiatric moments, most of us experience moving through the world as a self — as a cluster of body, feeling, and memory, of thought, desire, and practices, with a name and a continuity over time. I, Scott Neigh, am not and have never been some isolated entity that is separate from the world or from the greater *we* into/through which I am woven. But even so, while the boundaries that define me may be much less clear than commonly supposed,[3] I am nonetheless me, not someone else. *I* am the one who is experiencing, who is listening, who is doing. (And so, of course, are you, and so are they.)

As our selves move through the sensory landscape of the world, aspects of it impinge upon our awareness — we encounter people, we encounter the life of the more-than-human world, we encounter the world's physicality. We also encounter stories, images, analyses, and other kinds of knowledge produced by other people. As we have already explored, in the course of this, through all of our senses, we listen — we take in, we take up, we make meaning, and we act accordingly. In a way, our listening across all our senses to all these encounters that fill our days and nights *is* what the world is for us. They are the constantly shifting surface against which we bump that directs us this way rather than that; they are both our window into the world and the window through which the world enters us.

To start with, one thing is clear from even a cursory observation of everyday life: however the world works, whatever makes it like this rather than like that, it is not random. Which is not to say that it is never chaotic — it is. It is certainly not to suggest that it is never violent and terrible and unjust (as well as, sometimes, wonderful and nurturing and hopeful), because it is all these things. But the world is not a surrealist painting, an M.C. Escher drawing, or an exercise in the pure absence of form or order. Somehow, I am typing on an object made of raw materials brought together from who knows how many different countries, assembled from parts created in who knows how many more, and these words will one day be in a book that is in turn printed, circulated, promoted, bought, and read. Such extensive coordination could not dependably happen in a world that was random. I know, more or less, what to expect when I go out my door and walk through my city. I know, more or less, the things that police do, that paramedics do, that plumbers do, that banks do, and the ways that each enable and shape and limit and (for some — looking at you, cops and banks) end life. None of these things would be true if the world had no order to it, and none of them can be explained solely by looking at the level of individual character and action. There is something organized going on out there, whatever it might be.

complexity, reification, liberalism, and individualism

Most of us do not have good ways of thinking and talking about that organized something — the social world. I don't have a fully satisfying answer to why this is the case, but based on accounts of the world that seem to me to be robust and useful, I can identify at least a few relevant factors. Perhaps the most immediate is just that it is all rather complicated, in a way that is pretty much inevitable. As University of Manitoba scholar David Camfield puts it, "How societies work is not self-evident. Societies are complex, and appearances can be deceiving."[4] Moreover, as was said earlier, we can only listen directly to what is immediately around us, and a lot of how the social world works happens outside of that very limited venue. Again quoting Camfield, "To explain the forces that shape our personal experiences we need to understand things that we do not experience directly or transparently."[5] So of course it is not going to be easy.

Beyond that general and inescapable complexity, there are features specific to how our current social world is organized that make it even trickier. In various places through the book, I talk in different ways about how aspects of the social world can make it hard to listen and know. But when it comes to why we don't have good tools for thinking and naming (and listening to!) specifically the social character of the world around us, it feels useful to foreground how capitalism has shaped our world and our lives.

I'll get to some of the more intuitive aspects of this in a moment, but let me start with the one that seems the least obvious. There is a strand of Marxist thinking — based on allusions by Marx himself but really developed by Georg Lukács in the first half of the twentieth century[6] — that examines how, under capitalism, relations between people (a.k.a. social relations) are turned into relations among things, both in how they actually work and in how we are taught to understand them. This phenomenon, some argue, has become even more intense through the ways in which capitalism has been developing in the twentieth and twenty-first centuries.[7] This process is often called "reification," or sometimes "thingification" by the more plain-language inclined.[8]

What this means is that, under capitalism, "agency is given to profit, commodities, and things and not to the people who socially produce them."[9] We constantly hear on the news about stock markets and exchange rates and inflation, as if they have some concrete, autonomous existence and agency rather than recognizing that, underlying them, are the activities of human beings that have been organized, measured, and abstracted in various ways. It can be extremely difficult to talk about the world without falling into attributing agency to "society" or "the economy" or "the government," again in a way that erases that what we are actually talking about is people, doing things in particular ways. No amount of left exhortation can completely undo the way that our consciousness is organized into relating to the commodities we purchase as free-floating things that are detached from the many people whose doings created them. These manifestations of reification (and many others) make it difficult to understand and talk meaningfully about the social world.

More obviously, our current context makes it difficult to talk about the world in social ways because of the intense valorization of individualism in our culture. In using that term, I mean to capture the ways that we are taught to understand what goes on around us primarily in terms of what the individuals involved do or are or want. Good people and bad people, strong people and weak people, wise people and foolish people, people who have the right traits (values, character, in-born attributes, culture) and those who do not — thus do so much Sunday-dinner wisdom, internet commentary, and water-cooler chatter attempt to explain success and failure, health and harm, history and society, and pretty much everything else. Even in broadly progressive sources, you do not have to look far to find writing that attributes, say, the rapaciousness of corporations to the greed of individual capitalists or that reduces the harm and violence of racism, sexism, and homophobia to individually held incorrect ideas, bad choices, and/or moral turpitude. Similarly, we are surrounded by efforts to create change via pathways characterized as "empowerment" or "raising awareness" — that is, modes of change that are focused on shifting individual practices, feelings, or ideas.

Of course, individuals do cause harm, do (within the constraints of their lives) make choices, do sometimes change their path as a result of encountering new knowledge or a new sense of possibility. None of the preceding paragraph is to suggest that individuals should not be held accountable for their actions or that changes in what we do as individuals are never part of larger social change. The point is, though, that there is always more going on than that. The deeply embedded individualism in our culture makes it very hard for us to appreciate that fact and to understand the world as *social* rather than as a formless agglomeration of individuals.

This primacy of individualism is at least in part related to the ways in which life under capitalism shapes our perceptions of the world — that is, to currently hegemonic ideas. Capitalism, the dominant myth runs, is about individual freedom, in contrast with what existed before and what existed in other parts of the world for much of the twentieth century. There is far more wrong with that story than we have space to explore in detail here. It depends on caricatures of the pre-capitalist world and of those societies that have claimed (whether accurately or not) the mantle of "socialism." It depends on a narrow, specific, and harmful understanding of "freedom." And it exaggerates the possibility for individual autonomy open to the vast majority of people under capitalism by extolling a way of being in the world that is only ever possible for a narrow subset (mostly white men who own capital). Nonetheless, this story does capture something about how the shift towards capitalism disrupted existing social bonds — "All that is solid melts into air," as Marx and Engels wrote in 1848[10] — and created possibilities that for some people, in some moments are experienced as freedom, even as that depends on the immiseration of and violence done to others.

An important framework centred on a particular narrow conception of the individual blossomed alongside capitalism and developed into a range of analyses, politics, and accounts of the world, as well as social forms in the political realm, under the broad banner of "liberalism." I mean this not in the narrow, often party-political sense we encounter in everyday speech today, but as a broader system of thought and approach to organizing political life that underlies much of the common sense that many of us raised in North America bring to understanding the world, whether we self-identify politically as conservative, liberal in a narrow sense, or left. Liberalism has been widely critiqued, including for its complicity in empire, colonialism, and a range of other kinds of violence[11] and also for its emphasis on not just the individual, but the individual understood in a narrow and specific way, at the expense of the social.[12]

While there remains some debate about whether liberalism in its early years was as starkly individualistic as some of its critics claim, what is clear is the profound individualism embedded in the North Americanized liberalism of the twentieth and twenty-first centuries.[13] In the last fifty years or so, elites have been hard at work rolling back gains made by popular movements of ordinary people in the decades following the Second World War — a project often referred to at least by its opponents as "neoliberalism,"[14] which began just as a diverse array of popular movements in the 1960s and 1970s were opening up those earlier gains to many groups originally excluded from them. This powerful political trajectory has further entrenched and enhanced the atomization of society. As writer Pankaj Mishra observes, "Beginning in the 1990s ... the culture of individualism went universal,"[15] not only intensifying in many places where it was already strong but reaching into new corners of the globe. In the words of nehiyaw poet and scholar Billy-Ray Belcourt, we live in "a late-capitalist world in which individuality is a fetish, a mass object of desire, a political anthem."[16]

other accounts of the social

For all kinds of reasons, many of us do not have good access to ways of thinking and talking about the social world. After all, it is the dominant stories around us that most often inform our common sense and that most of us are able to draw upon, and they are usually some contradictory and unhelpful mix of reification, individualism, and mystificatory affirmation of an oppressive status quo. However, it is possible to find accounts of the social world that differ in ways small and large from liberal individualism. People who are part of communities that face significant ongoing struggle, for example, or who are active in social movements are likely to encounter ways of thinking about the social world that go beyond the dominant mainstream stories in important respects.[17] Other people, who are not part of such collective spaces, can learn about non-dominant accounts of the social world on their own through seeking them out and listening. That may take the form of talking to people, of consuming alternative media, of reading books, and so on. While postsecondary education is not accessible to lots of people and can be a powerful way in which all sorts of oppressive understandings are reproduced, nonetheless there are still corners of universities where the people fortunate enough to be there can gain access to a wide range of ways of understanding the social world.

The specific accounts beyond the mainstream that are easiest to name tend to be associated today with university contexts. That does not mean they are the most important or that they are taken up by the most people — they just tend to be visible because the institutions where they are produced or claimed are socially prominent and are in the business of articulating and naming ideas. Any university bookstore will have textbooks with chapter titles like "Karl Marx," "Max Weber," "Symbolic Interactionism," "Feminist Theories," and "Race, Racism, and the Construction of Racial Otherness."[18] Such books present tiny glimpses into rich, diverse, and often internally contradictory traditions that represent constellations of interrelated accounts of the social world. We could come up with many more examples, often named as a particular school of thought or after a prominent thinker. The risk in naming these examples is that it feeds into the common assumption that accounts of the social world that challenge dominant ways of thinking are only or inherently academic in character. In fact, some of the most important — including three of the chapter titles listed — emerged from contexts of collective struggle by ordinary people and were only later taken up in postsecondary settings. Many continue to have resonance, albeit complicated and contested, across broad non-academic contexts today. Often, the accounts of the social world most actively relevant to collective struggle in a given moment are much harder to pin down, name, and define in that moment.

The abundance of different ways of thinking about the social once you break out of the narrow field that dominates public life in North America presents its own challenge for those of us trying to understand and change the world. Who and what in this confusing breadth should we believe and use to ground our actions? Accounts of the social world can be wildly divergent, often contradicting each other in important ways, or at least painting pictures that seem to have little to do with each other. Many incorporate problematic elements of dominant accounts. Even if they differ in some ways from dominant accounts, that is no guarantee that they will be able to do what we need them to. If the recent growth in conspiratorial and far-right accounts of the world tells us anything, it is that just because something rails against the status quo is no reason to give it the time of day.

In the context of that abundance, most of us, most of the time, do not move through the world guided by an all-encompassing, fully complete, radically coherent, singular account of the social world. Partly, this is because our accounts themselves are inevitably incomplete. Our capacity to theorize the world never matches the world itself, so the accounts we produce always incorporate limitations, imperfections, failures. Any given account is likely to reflect what matters in the context in which it was developed, what it is expected to explain or do, and what existing understandings (and misunderstandings) it is drawing on. Certainly, standpoint and all the ways knowledge is always situated get built into analyses, stories, and other ways of understanding the social world.

Beyond that, we draw on different accounts to make sense of different things, to guide us in different contexts, to organize different parts of our lives. If you are deciding how to deal with gendered power in your family, it might be useful to start from different accounts of the social world than if you are trying to figure out why the auto industry employs so many fewer people in Ontario today than it did a few decades ago. In either case, you might operate under the same overarching framework as you listen — maybe it is something clearly nameable, like feminism, or maybe it is the accumulation of stories you have heard from your grandparents and other elders in your life — but in dealing with each scenario, you still might benefit from listening to theorizing, to thinking, to knowledge that is grounded in a range of other specific accounts. Finally, this is also just a feature of how people work. We aren't consistent. We are a product of lots of different influences. Our actions in one set of circumstances might reflect one kind of account of the social world and in other circumstances reflect a very different one, and we may not even be aware of it. This is no less true for those of us who strongly identify with one specific account. In all sorts of different ways, to be human is to be a complicated, jumbled mess.

dealing with multiplicity

All of us already have practices for dealing with the multiplicity of accounts of the social world that are out there. They may not be very effective practices, and we may not be particularly conscious of them, but we have them. I say that with such confidence because they are exactly the same practices that we have for dealing with everything else. We take in, we take up, we assess, we make meaning. We put the new in relation with our existing knowledge, with the accounts of the world that already guide us, and we do the things we might do with any other new knowledge. Sure, we may or may not be used to thinking explicitly about different accounts of the world, and the overarching frameworks we are already invested in are more stubbornly resistant to change than more peripheral sorts of knowledge. But, still, when we encounter and listen to some account of the world that is new to us, we inevitably do *something*.

 Some of the ways we are brought face-to-face with a new account of the social world — a class, a book, a proselytizing friend — spell it all out explicitly. This forces us to be a bit more deliberate in dealing with this new account, a bit more conscious that we are in fact confronting something new, and it is more likely to give us the opportunity to appreciate how this new account differs from that with which we are already familiar. In other situations, even if it is obvious that an account we are not used to is involved, the details might be much less clear. Let's go back to the example of the decline of the auto industry in Ontario. Say you read a scholarly article on the topic. As you read that article, you are encountering specific claims about a specific set of circumstances, but you are also encountering the account of the world that is grounding those claims — let's call that account "Marxist political economy." To a limited extent, it probably explains that grounding explicitly. But it is just a single article, and it would take entire books to fully characterize the account. Plus, it is not unusual for writing of that sort to presume a certain level of familiarity with its premises. Mostly, it would probably combine pointing to the account that grounds it through references and just embedding it implicitly in what it is saying. So, the article does not give you everything you need to understand the account.

A lot of the time, the nuts and bolts of the account, and perhaps even the fact that you are dealing with such a thing at all, are even less clear. Say you read a novel, or watch a movie, or listen to a story that draws on some non-dominant account of the world but doesn't even name it, let alone explain it. Or say you read a news piece about a grassroots direct-action group mobilizing in support of Black lives and against police violence, and their actions are informed by a particular abolitionist account of the world. That account is embedded in the actions that it guides and also in the article, both because the article talks about the actions and because the journalist may provide at least some minimal opportunity for the abolitionists to explain their choices. But the account's presence and character may not be easily visible to you.

Particularly when accounts are less obvious, but not only then, we may just straight-up fail (or refuse) to notice them. Or we may recognize that we are faced with accounts of the world that differ from our own but make no effort to engage with or understand them. Or we may find ways to take them up that distort them, to make them fit with accounts of the world that we are already invested in — this can happen in lots of different ways, of course, but, given its prominence in our culture, it is perhaps most common for people to read other accounts into liberal individualism.

Our uptake and integration of new accounts of the social world, when it occurs at all, is complex and partial. Think again about the Marxist article about Ontario's auto industry and consider what you might make of it if you had never read anything like it before. As you apply all the steps of listening we have talked about — with whatever degree of gut-level reaction or explicit rigour, grounded in whatever standpoint you work from — you are assessing this new-to-you account and deciding what you want to do with it. Maybe you reject it in its entirety. Maybe you have some mixture of interest and questions, enthusiasm and uncertainty. But let's assume the other extreme, that you are impressed with how able this article is to explain features of the social world relevant to the topic, and you adopt some of it. No matter how favourable your response, however, the ways in which you take in, take up, and make meaning from that account are inevitably going to be partial — as I said, one little article cannot be enough to convey the entirety of that account, and listening always happens in uneven ways. Even under the most optimal of circumstances imaginable, *maybe* some elements of Marxist political economy begin to inform your words and actions in some ways, in some contexts, but there are going to be serious limits to how far that extends, and it is likely going to require a lot more reading, thinking, and acting to get to that point. There are lots of other domains of life and aspects of the world where it is not at all clear what it could even mean for our words and actions to be informed by Marxist political economy. With any account of the world and any degree of familiarity, there will always be unevenness and limits and contexts in which other accounts predominate.

grounding in experience

It is worth reflecting on why it is useful to assess the new accounts of the social world we encounter. The goal is not to arrive at a final, singular One True Way. Given what we have already said about the inevitable partiality of accounts of the social world, it can't be. Rather, different accounts exist in relation with each other, with those who hold them, and with the world they claim to explain. It is a matter of figuring out what each account can and cannot do, the contexts in which it is useful versus those in which it is not, the ways it helps us understand the world, make decisions, and live our lives versus the ways in which it falls short. No single account can do everything, so what can this one do?

Given that we already have practices for dealing with new-to-us accounts of the world, even if we haven't thought much about them before, my goal is not to offer you practices to replace what you already do. After all, we can only start from where we are and shift our listening practices through a recursive journey of listening, learning, and listening some more. What I want to do instead is offer a few practices to add to your existing repertoire.

My first suggestion is about attention. As I said, it can be easy to ignore the ways in which accounts are embedded in words and actions that do not make them explicit. So, pay closer attention to that. Make it a matter of course to ask what this news report, this piece of fiction, this activist intervention implies about how the people involved understand the social world.[19] Look for clues. Deduce. Investigate. I think it is also useful for us to pay closer attention to our own practices. What are we doing as we take in, take up, and make meaning, and as we engage with new accounts of the world? What about those practices might we want to change?

The other practices that could be useful are all related, in one way or another, to using everyday experience to assess accounts of the social world. We can take our own experiences and those of other people as a test or grounding. At its most basic, this can mean that when we are evaluating an account, we can ask, does it deal with this experience that I or other people have had? If not, why not? If it does, how does it do so? This would mean not just thinking critically about the account but also about the experience, how we have made meaning from it, and how we have put it into narrative. Just because the account we are considering does not explain or predict or explore a given experience is not intrinsically a reason to stop listening to what it has to say, but it is a basis for saying, hey, there's something missing here and for figuring out exactly what that means.

In applying this test, obviously one crucial starting point is our own experience. This is doubly true for people who face oppressions of various kinds and whose experiences are less likely to be taken seriously in the context of dominant accounts of the social world. But it is also important, especially but definitely not only for those of us with relative privilege, to look beyond that. Accounts of the social world, to be meaningful and robust, not only need to deal with my experience, they need to deal with the experiences of people situated differently than me.

I know I have had one kind of experience with the police, as a middle-class, white, cisgender man. As someone who has engaged in grassroots political work, including at times direct action and civil disobedience, I have also had some experiences of police that are a little different than many middle-class white guys. But I know that many other people, for instance many Black and Indigenous people, have *very* different experiences of police and policing than I do, in general and in the context of grassroots political work; thus, an account of the social world should provide ways of understanding why and how this is the case. Of course, just because an account claims to do that says nothing about how well or accurately it does so, and attending to experience does not provide all the answers — theory and investigation beyond the everyday matter too, as do the practices of listening and knowing we would bring to bear on anything else. But, still, valuing everyday experience and using it as a way to check new accounts can be a useful resource and an important starting point.

characteristics of the world

Another practice that can be useful for navigating the multiplicity of accounts of the social world is figuring out some key characteristics of the world that we think any robust account should reflect. These are things that emerge from our own and others' experience across lots of different contexts and from accounts that have been heavily grounded through those experiences. They are broader and more general than individual experiences but are just single features of the world rather than attempts themselves to be full accounts. We can assess an account of the social world by asking whether or not it includes such features and by favouring accounts that do. Of course, even if they do not, that does not automatically mean we should discount them. But in such a case, we can deliberately listen to and take up that account in ways that read the feature in question into it or that at least put it into relation with that feature. All of this is potentially risky — it would be easy to use this tool to justify biases that have no basis in reality — but also potentially useful if done with care.

There are lots of different ways that you could apply this, and I'm sure there are lots of different possible characteristics that would be valid and useful. Below are five features I have come up with, which emerge from my own efforts over the last three decades to learn about the social world. I have already mentioned the first, but I repeat it here because in some ways it is a key premise for this whole conversation — that the social world is *organized* and is not just a formless fluid mass of individuals like water molecules in a glass. It has internal shape, it has regularity, it has perceptible form, it has ways in which things happen that are distinct from ways in which they do not and cannot. None of which is to presume anything about what that form is, how it happens, or how it works, just that we can reasonably suppose that it exists and that the world is, in some way, socially organized.

Next, and perhaps most important in a political sense, the world as it currently exists is *unjust*. Any account of the social world must give us tools to name and engage meaningfully with that fact, whether directly or indirectly. I know that the world is unjust, and in many respects terribly so, through listening to both my own experiences and those of people situated differently than me — especially the latter — and from the clear evidence that those experiences are not random but happen in predictable, organized, and systemic ways.

A robust and convincing account of the social world must also recognize that it is *complex*. There can be a lot to this, but the element I am most interested in is another that we have already touched on — the world inevitably escapes full explanation by our accounts, exceeds our attempts to theorize it, overflows the categories that we try to impose on it. We still need accounts and categories as part of naming our experiences and naming the world in order to change it. But recognizing complexity is about how we hold those categories and stories, how we understand their relation to the world and to people's lives. It is about refusing the ways in which they are used to police, to limit, to rule. Even on the left, I have encountered many people committed to a flat, abstracted account of the world that denies complexity and speaks in broad categories that trample over the inherently nuanced, difficult, and contradictory character of life as it is actually lived, rather than inviting all that in. But given the work I have done over the years, I find it mystifying that anyone can deny how life and the world can never be contained by the categories and the stories we use to understand them.

The social world is also *investigable*. That means that we can listen to the world and come to know things about it — what is and isn't happening, how it works, how it got to be that way. Not everything, of course, and not all the time, and there is much to discuss and debate about how best to do it and where the limits lie. But, regularly and substantively, we can listen to the world and learn. I know this from doing it myself and from many, many encounters with other people's efforts to do it. Saying that it is investigable means it is not just possible to listen and derive meaning that is unique to the person listening — though that happens too — but to listen and to learn things that predict or explain or account for what is happening in the world in a shared, replicable way.

Finally, the social world and all of us in it are *interconnected.* The first sense in which I mean that is through the practical, material ways the shape of my life is a product of the same dense global web of relationships as yours, as hers over there, as them around the world. All of us are part of the *same* social world. My life is radically different from a young single mother on welfare in Helsinki, a working-class queer anarchist in Cairo, or a peasant living outside of Jakarta or in the jungles of Chiapas, but the things that shape their lives and the things that shape my life are interconnected. A little investigation reveals that the same powerful states and global institutions and the same flows of capital, goods, and information are involved.

I also mean interconnection in a sense related to the increasingly popular idea of "intersectionality." Contemporary use of the cluster of ideas related to this term can sometimes be at quite a remove from their radical origins,[20] and debates about them regularly fail to recognize their roots in accounts of the social world that are starkly at odds with the liberal framework into which they are often read today. The term "intersectionality" itself was coined by African American feminist legal scholar Kimberlé Crenshaw,[21] but its roots lie in earlier traditions of grassroots Black feminist thought and practice. It is an expression of Audre Lorde's famous observation that "there is no such thing as a single-issue struggle because we do not live single-issue lives."[22] And the Combahee River Collective, a formation of radical Black lesbian feminists in the 1970s, wrote, "[We] see as our particular task the development of integrated analysis and practice based upon the fact that the major systems of oppression are interlocking."[23] Black feminist sociologist Patricia Hill Collins describes this aspect of the social world as the "matrix of domination," which she uses to "describe this overall social organization within which intersecting oppressions originate, develop, and are contained."[24] These overlapping (but not identical) analyses get at how the many injustices and axes of oppression that pervade our world do not exist independently of each other but in complex, interconnected ways.

keeping people at the centre

Finally, it is possible to set out in a more deliberate way to learn things about the world — to investigate, to listen with particular kinds of knowing in mind — in ways that generate knowledge that remains firmly a part of the realm of our everyday experience and so can, in the same spirit, also be used as a way to ground and test accounts of the social world. So, what I want to do is talk a little bit about one particular account and its associated approach for making knowledge as a basis for doing this. I am not presenting it to supersede whatever other accounts you happen to find useful — it is not an attempt to tell you to abandon the words of Marx or Fanon, Butler or Monture-Angus, your grandfather or your radical collective, Piepzna-Samarasinha or Kaba, Foucault or the anonymous organizer whom you just heard interviewed. I have no more desire to give up the wisdom, the analytical power, and the potential for social transformation found in all of those than you do. But I am suggesting that the account that I am about to present can be an additional rich resource for assessing and making use of whatever others you value.

This account of the world comes from the work of the late Canadian feminist sociologist Dorothy Smith and the approach to sociology she called "institutional ethnography."[25] In her understanding — which is related to the analysis of reification touched on above — a lot of scholarly work and other writing about the social world "displaces people, displaces their activities, displaces the social relations and organization of their doings"[26] in a way deeply embedded in how the discourse and practices of sociology are themselves socially organized.[27] A crucial part of her work was to create an approach to understanding the social world that did *not* displace people and their socially organized relations and doings — in other words, an account that emerged from and stayed grounded in people's everyday and everynight experiences, even while working to understand features of the social world, particularly the *how* of it, that exist beyond the everyday.

Smith's awareness of this disjuncture came from noticing a profound difference between the kind of consciousness she experienced in the course of her work as a graduate student in university contexts and the kind of consciousness she experienced while at home with her children — a disjuncture that was about the ways in which her activities in those two settings were organized. At home, she was engaged with the world immediately around her in all of its local, material specificity, whereas she experienced "a practice of subjectivity in the university that excluded the local and bodily from its field."[28] This, she realized, had implications for the knowledge produced in that context, and it became a core feminist commitment for her to elaborate a way of investigating the social world that "begins in the local actualities of people's lives" and keeps them at the centre even while mapping the extra-local ways in which people's doings are coordinated.[29]

In order to understand the institutions that shape our lives — the "relations of ruling," as Smith sometimes refers to them — you start from experience, your own or someone else's. You don't just start from any moment, though, but from one that reflects a particular kind of disjuncture between different ways of knowing the world in the context of the institution you are studying. On the one side, you have knowledge generated by people who are part of that institution in the course of its work. These are abstract approaches, explanations, ideas, ways of thinking that constitute "a set of procedures used to know theoretically, categorically, a social world with a view to administering it."[30] On the other, you have the local, material specificity of the lives of the ordinary people who are subject to that institution. All of us have had the experience of bumping into some bureaucratic something that no doubt makes perfect sense from the perspective of the bureaucracy and is useful in administering whatever it is the bureaucracy administers, but that is ridiculous when considered in the context of a real person's actual life. This kind of disjuncture is not just annoying or amusing, however, but is often deeply enmeshed in the harms that systems of power inflict on people. The perspective of the people facing those harms can be a crucial starting point to investigate how such regimes of ruling are socially organized.

This is how Smith uses the idea of standpoint — you begin your investigation from the standpoint of, say, the social assistance recipient facing harmful and arbitrary demands from the bureaucracy or the Black youth being subjected to police harassment. That starting point allows you to get a more thorough and robust understanding of the institutions and relations of ruling in a way that will not be possible if you begin your investigation from within the perspectives offered by that institution, though you incorporate knowledge generated from those standpoints as well. In the context of the less formal way I am thinking about her approach here, that means that while any robust account of policing should be able to explain why police have the experiences they have, and why I, middle-class white guy that I am, have the experiences that I do, it really should start from the experiences of those who are most starkly subject to the harms of policing. This is not a moral or straightforwardly political "should" but is premised on the reality that starting there will result in knowing more and better.

In investigating how the social world is put together, you stick to the kinds of practical, material causes and effects that can be observed or deduced in the context in which the experience is taking place, i.e., at the level of everyday life. As you follow those chains of causality and relationality, you find out that the experience you started from is a result of other people doing things in their own local settings and of networks of relationships among people. In doing this, you discover certain basic kinds of things almost always play a role in shaping people's experiences, across most contexts. Smith emphasizes the role of texts in coordinating what we do — policies, laws, regulations, and so on — but images, more diffuse ideologies, and probably other things can play a similar role. We take up such texts and activate them ourselves, or we have to navigate the reality that the people around us — the police officer, the manager, the teacher — are doing so. These texts or images or ideologies are in turn produced by other people in other places engaging in their own socially organized practices. One element of understanding the world based on this account is, therefore, going from the recognition that, say, some oppressive thing is happening in your workplace, to recognizing the role of employment law and company policy in producing that circumstance, to investigating how that policy was made in the first place. In theory, you can start from a moment of disjuncture, then trace through practical, investigable causal chains at the level of everyday experience and map out the world in a practical way that stays grounded in our lives. You can pursue these chains of doing, of encounter, of coordination to understand how pretty much anything was socially produced.

I want to emphasize again that I am not trying to replace whatever accounts you already find useful but to offer ways of knowing the world that can help you assess, enrich, and strengthen them — and, yes, sometimes change them. It is a way to get at how things work at the level of our everyday experience, which we can then take and ask, well, what does this other account of the world say about that. For those of us not likely to engage in the kinds of formal investigations that can emerge from these ideas, it can still feed into a sensibility that guides our informal knowledge production and our sense of the *how* of the social world, which we can in turn use in engaging with the other accounts that we come across.

the social world and listening

As you may have already guessed, there is one more reason why I wanted to share this way of understanding the social world and how it is put together: it helps make clear the central role played by listening. At every stage, the mechanics of the social world this account explores and maps — the way it actually happens in practice — involve the responsiveness that is listening. When we encounter another person and respond to what they do, to what they might do, to what we fear they will do, to what they have done in the past, it is through listening to their words and actions that our own are in turn shaped. When our doings are coordinated by a policy in our workplace, by a traffic law, by an unspoken but fiercely enforced social norm, by an image, by a story, it is through listening that we take those up and turn their content into action. We take in, take up, and make meaning from what is said to us, from what is done to us, from what we observe around us, from what we anticipate about what might happen next, from all our sensory inputs, and we act in return. Constant reciprocal listening is the basis of any engagement, any interconnection, any relation, and most chains of causality that pass through human agency.

This means that listening is not just an individual action, practice, capacity, or trait. It means that listening is not just an important part of interpersonal relating, of the substance of a friendship or how you, I, and they might become in some sense *we*. It means that listening is absolutely central to how our social world as a whole works. Even if that listening is not named in a given account, when you dig under the surface and try to think through what people are doing, and why, and how, at the level at which they are actually living their lives, listening is inevitably a key part of how it is all put together. Our collective capacity to be responsive, to listen, is a key part of how our lives are shaped, of how actions in one local context might have impacts in many others, of how the world is woven.

part 2

listening's reach and limits

chapter four

the scream and the murmur

When I listen, what do I hear,[1] what do I see, what do I feel? I, Scott Neigh, the author, me — when I open myself up to the hubbub and the voices, what does my listening bring me, in the context of this organized, unjust, complex, investigable, interconnected social world? My listening, like anybody's, is an ever-changing swirl of stimuli and sensations, a rush of colours and tones, experiences and words. My listening is pleasurable, painful, informative, boring. It connects me, it shapes me, it helps me do, it helps me know. But within all of that, I think there is a crucial essence to my listening, a recurrent core to what it tells me about the world and about myself. Sometimes, at least — an important caveat to which I return in the next chapter — I hear screams and I hear murmurs.

In the first instance, the scream is something we do. It is the scream that John Holloway wrote of: "Faced with the mutilation of human lives by capitalism, a scream of sadness, a scream of horror, a scream of anger, a scream of refusal: NO."[2] The scream may sound more like a grumble, a roar, a sob, a dissonance, a frustrated groan. Some of it is in response to what we face ourselves, what we feel directly on our bodies, what is taken from us every day. Some is a response to what we observe — the stories from friends and from the news, the social media posts and the tearful phone calls, the open letters and the careful scholarship. It erupts from the overwhelming harms, felt and witnessed, along so many axes of exploitation and oppression. Who among us can bear to face the world in all its worsening brutality and *not* grumble, roar, sob — or, distilled to its purest form, scream in sadness and rage and refusal?

It is this scream that is our starting point for knowing and doing. It is a "scream of rejection-and-longing,"[3] a "scream of horror-and-hope."[4] It rejects the world's denial of our dignity, asserts that dignity in the face of its denial, and yearns for a better world. It does not depend on us having it all figured out, on being able to name it all, on knowing how to get to that better future. It is a visceral cry that surely, surely, surely, we can do better. When Holloway writes of this scream, it is of our own scream, of the scream we collectively participate in, as a starting point for how we orient ourselves to our violent, oppressive world. But in this chapter, I am writing not about participating in the scream but listening to it. Yes, I scream, but I also hear the screams of others.

I hear your horror and hope. I witness your rejection of the current world and longing for a better one. I see your dignity thrust in the face of its denial. Most of all, when I hear your scream, I hear *you*. I hear a voice, a self.[5] Screams, after all, are not a vocalization for subtleties — I may hear the broad shape of our violent world's denial of your dignity, the outline of the self you assert despite it, but mostly I hear that you are there, that you exist, that you refuse not-being, that you overflow whatever the world tells you that you must be. When I hear your scream, it is not in itself an invitation to listen further, but it is a signal that listening is possible, that listening must be part of anything that might lead to a *we* that struggles together against indignity.

I also hear a constant murmur. It is all the sounds of life at its most ordinary — the burble of the stream of the everyday, the most unremarkable bangs and clangs and laughs and mutters of the sensory landscape that surrounds us. When I sit writing on my front porch, I hear the wheels of a suitcase bumping over sidewalk cracks as its grim-faced owner pulls it along. When I am in a cafe, I see people huddled over laptops and sipping their drinks, and I hear last year's pop hit, the rumble of roasted beans being ground, fragments of four conversations, and the constant noises of mugs and spoons and plates in use. You might dimly hear two co-workers arguing about a TV show or the white-noise hiss of a baby monitor that will soon turn into either happy coos or angry roars.

These are the sounds of life happening without fanfare. They are, in their own way, also an assertion of dignity. Rather than the dignity of defiance in the face of its denial, the murmur is the sound of the living of dignity despite its denial. The world is awful, violence and oppression are legion, yet lunch needs to be made, nappies need to be changed, tables need to be bussed, orders need to be filled. Moreover, sometimes these are the sounds of the everyday success we nonetheless have in finding pleasure, meaning, joy.

A murmur is quiet and indistinct. It is enough to draw our notice, perhaps even enough to hold our attention. It may hint at the shape of the life from which it emanates, but it is only a hint — a few words, a tone of voice, the sound of the bustle of living. It may gesture broadly, but it provides no details. It is, as with the scream, a *self* that is heard and a sign that there is more to hear, but not in itself an invitation to listen further.

All of that is to put it in a figurative way, of course. It is not necessarily clear what all this means for concrete instances of listening. Take the suitcase wheels on the sidewalk: I live on a residential street not too far from an emergency shelter for women. Hearing/seeing that woman walk by, suitcase in tow, I am not sure whether it is a murmur, a scream, or both that I hear. Certainly, it is a quiet sound of everyday living, and that might be all it is — a trip to visit a friend that has nothing to do with the nearby shelter, an unremarkable, everyday instance of the living of dignity despite its ongoing denial by patriarchal social relations and not anything more immediate or sharp. Or it might well be an anguished manifestation of "No!", a refusal of acute misery, and a yearning for something better. I'm more interested in bringing these figures down to earth than continuing to explore them purely as figures, but it seems likely that were I to proceed in this vein, I would discover that they are not as distinct as they seem, not poles in a binary, but rather that every murmur contains a scream and every scream, a murmur. Rebellion, after all, is not some exceptional thing but something happening all the time, all around us — as the Zapatistas say, "We are perfectly ordinary people, therefore rebels."[6]

listening in practice

Practically speaking, then, what do I hear? Yes, talk of screams and murmurs is all well and good, but in the scenes of my days and nights, my weeks and months, what do I actually hear, see, smell, taste, feel?

I sit in my backyard working on my laptop under bright warm sun. I hear the faint rush of the breeze through the trees, and I see the leaves dance. I see our home, a fence, flowers and plants. I hear a bird chirping in the tree above me. I hear cars and cars and cars on the major street a block to the south.

Or I put my tray down on a table in the food court in the downtown mall. There are the noises of commerce, the hiss of frying, the bangs of cooking and serving, occasionally the low rumble of a cart being rolled to empty a garbage can. But mostly, this space is filled with voices. It isn't even all that full, but the sound is like a quilt sewn together from countless, ever-changing fragments of talk. I see a context that, other than the important and troubling fact that it is privately owned, is what urban public space is supposed to be like. It is a place where a great breadth of humanity — living so many different intersections of the axes that shape us — swirl around each other, paths overlapping and intertwining or just passing by. It is pervaded by the same oppression and resistance we find everywhere, what with the wealthy white gymnastics mom oozing contempt for the hoi-polloi next to her in line, the security guards hassling that homeless guy over by the bathroom entrance, and so on, but it is still a remarkable, vibrant crossing point for many, many lives. Through it all flows a lively current of dignity and joy — a delightful sense of selves, living.

Or I stop and get out of the car to fill it with gas. There is a breeze, not heard but felt. There are other people around — driving through the plaza parking lot where this station is located, pumping gas into their own cars, visible through the window in the attached convenience store. I select the grade of gas I need. The display blinks. I wait. It blinks some more. And finally, a beep. I can pump now. As I do, I think about that beep. On one level, it is a noise like many others — a powerfully ordinary aural marker of the technology that fills our lives. I know that this specific beep happened most proximally because one of the workers inside the convenience store received a notification, glanced in my direction to ensure no purpose more nefarious than the purchase of fossil fuel, and clicked something. That click told the machinery that it was okay to begin releasing gasoline. It also told the machinery to beep.

I hear this in the beep because of what I already know. I know this because for a stretch of time in about 1999, in a station on the other side of the city, I was the person at the other end of that beep. The gas station I worked at didn't have a full-sized convenience store but instead just a little kiosk. It was a terrible job. The pay was minimum wage and the hours irregular, but beyond that there was a complete lack of trust in employees. You had to count the entire inventory of the kiosk at the beginning and end of each shift, and any mismatch with the till was deducted from your pay. Ostensibly, this was to keep you motivated to surveil the customers and make sure they weren't palming a bag of Skittles or a pack of Juicy Fruit while you gave them change for their gas purchase, but it was pretty clear that it was really about making sure you, yourself, didn't augment your meagre wages by liberating a few empty calories. Of course, you were on camera the entire time too — "for your own protection," no doubt. Most galling of all was the franchise owner, a thirty-something white woman with trust-fund wealth who styled herself as progressive and enlightened, but whose complete ease with the fact that she deserved her money and power while those who worked for her had little of either was so total and firm that it had a certain innocence about it.

Hearing the beep triggered in me a brief experience of listening that was complex and layered. Though we are often not aware of it, this is how our listening works pretty much all the time. In the most obvious layer, what we sense tells us something direct and immediate about the input that has bumped into our senses. In this case, the beep is a product of technology and a prompt to continue, analogous to many other beeps in many other contexts. At the same time, the incoming stimuli also evoke whatever relevant broader knowledge we already hold about source, context, and meaning. We hear not just the immediate sensory input but something of where it came from, what it is doing, what else it is attached to. Some of that is grounded and sure, some more speculative and imaginative. So sometimes, based on past living and past listening, the current moment's listening can extend, in a hazy and partial way, into the dense and multifaceted chains of relations and practices producing whatever I'm listening to. Such listening beyond the immediate can be experienced as a sequence of deliberate steps, including reasoning and deduction. But often, we do this as a single thing, a sensing in and of the moment and simultaneously, through the moment, of hazy shapes of the world that produced it, or at least a few of them — a wash of affects, a range of possible circumstances, a fuzzy tangle of relations, a cluster of likely practices. Either way, listening to a beep can mean listening, in a precarious and limited way, to the social world as it precedes, produces, and surrounds that beep.

In doing this, we can most definitely be wrong. Our existing knowledge can extend our listening in ways that mislead us, that hear things that are not there or mishear what is there. Certainly, more deliberate reflection can identify more than listening in the moment, and the kind of investigation and mobilization of our knowledge discussed in the last chapter can do much more than that. Mostly, though, we don't even try to do those sorts of things, and I certainly do nothing of the kind when I hear that beep at the gas station. But, still, even without all of that, in the moment of listening, I not only know that I can pump my gas, but I also — without effort or investigation — hear echoes of the low-wage employment relation and work practices of the workers in the convenience store. I hear long, boring shifts. I hear lousy wages and conditions. I hear high turnover, surveillance. I hear these things while others might not, just as I know in many other circumstances, others hear things that completely escape me. It is not just reminders of isolated experiences from my own past I hear but, because of what I already know, I hear echoes of widely shared experiences of precarity and indignity, of pervasive injustice, of the social here and now, all layered into that brief sound.[7]

So, as I get into my car, I can think back to writing in my backyard and to hanging out in the mall food court. There, too, I was sensing more than just evidence of physical movement that sent vibrations through the air, more than just light bouncing from surfaces. There, too, my existing knowledge allowed me to listen to the traces of social relations echoing through the sensory moments. At the grandest scale, the endless roar of vehicles heard from my hammock is the sound of the global fossil fuel industry, of imperial wars for oil, and of the ongoing climate crisis but also of the everyday murmur of ten thousand lives. The birdsong is a lingering trace that points towards a past before this land had a city slapped down on top of it — and so, also, to all manner of colonial and capitalist violence and to resistance. The many voices and faces in the food court point to the broad sweep of social relations, to the violence of borders and the violence of poverty, to (once again) the scream and the murmur, and the living and thriving and dignity and joy that people still relentlessly manage despite the state of the world.

conversation

As much as we can sometimes hear in the overall sensory landscape of everyday life, where I learn the most that is new-to-me about the world, where the scream and the murmur are clearest, is as I listen to other people. As discussed earlier, voices (both internal and external) and a range of other kinds of emanations originating with people reach us in many ways. But the simplest context, perhaps the model for all the rest, is conversation.

I listen to the words another person speaks to me, and I learn. It is the words that allow this, but it is not just the words — yes, the knowledge the speakers have generated about their own lives, how they have assessed and evaluated and chosen to communicate it, but also the tone, the pause, the silence, the breath. It is how they feel, how I feel, the space we have built together in this moment. It is the interplay with what was said five minutes ago and five years ago. It is my sedimented sense of them and their lives, the ever-evolving imagining of person and context, and every flicker of nuance and richness that imagining can draw from their words as I hear them. Most of all, as with the gas pump beep, it is what these words and pauses and tones and silences carry with them, in this case much more generously because they are not a fleeting mechanical noise but rich communication laden with life and meaning.

What I hear is not just the semantic content of abstract words, but the holus-bolus complexity dragged along by sounds emitted from a fleshy throat, carried across air and into fleshy ears.[8] For others, that complexity is carried by light between hands and eyes. In all such encounters, at their best, the engagement is not just with words, but with a self, a person, a whole complex being. Even when it is all mediated by text or image and flesh is at a remove, still the fact that it is embodied people at either end of the relation, and that we exist in our own messy concrete webs of sociality, means that there is more there than the obvious content, if only we can hear it.

A long-ago example: It was a heavy-hot, chrome-glinting day, one of the first of the year. The wide, car-filled road lined with businesses with suburban-style parking lots made it feel like a part of the city where pedestrians were not welcome, even though it was just down from the university. We were walking to my friend's apartment. I have never done well with heat, and I may have grumbled about it. What I do remember is her expressing her own ambivalence about the time of year. In her case, it was not about the weather per se, which she quite liked for the recreational opportunities it afforded. Rather, as she wearily and matter-of-factly told me, it was because making this walk twice each day while wearing clothes suitable for the weather — I remember she was wearing a sundress that day — meant she got cat-called a few times a week. Now, I was no stranger even that many years ago to the quotidian awfulness that women experience from men, but this particular manifestation came as a surprise. It certainly should not have, but it did. I think I expressed that surprise ("Really???"), and she scoffed (more gently than I deserved) and reaffirmed her experience, and the conversation moved on. The obvious content of her words was her experience, and that is about it. Like I said, we did not linger, we did not dissect, we did not analyze — at least not in that conversation. Yet even without all of that, those words carried with them a substantial, powerful *more*. They revealed, implied, carried-with. Whether she meant them to or not, her words offered a peek into her inner life and into a fragment of the social world that had shaped her experience.

Think of this *more* as echoes. Not echoes in the sense of delayed repetition but like the echoes of bats or submarines sensing the world through reflected sound, though less precise. Or think of this *more* as a flash, a bright light suddenly there and suddenly gone as you walk through an unknown place in the dark — the glimpse it offers is partial, incomplete, fleeting, and probably not enough on its own to stop you from jamming your toe or barking your shin, but it is a glimpse nonetheless. Think of this *more* as a shape that forms in your mind, as an impression, as — if you can bear the sensorily mixed metaphor — a wavery shadow cast by a self and its world through the prism of a voice. It tells you something about how the person is put together and about the world as it exists around them.

what i hear

Let me say it again: Ideally, first and foremost, when I am listening as I want to be listening, as I know I should be listening, as I try to listen, as I often do listen (but not always), I am not just listening to words, I am not just gaining knowledge. Rather, I am listening to entire, rich, complex selves, I am speaking in response, and I am building relationship. As I listen, as I engage with these rich, complex selves, and also as I listen in contexts where the engagement is shallower but nonetheless substantive, I learn, I gradually change.

Of course, regularly and inevitably, listening fails — at times, it fails painfully, it fails profoundly — and I come back to that in the next chapter. But, also regularly and inevitably, listening succeeds. It often tells me things important and real about those to whom I am listening, about the world, and about myself. When I listen well, deliberately signalled in words or carried along in the *more* of it all, I often sense something sharp and urgent. I hear the scream and the murmur. I hear power and resistance, domination and struggle, attempts to steal joy and efforts to hold it. Moreover, they are not rare, they are not few, they are not exceptional — I hear them all around. Urgently, they call for solidarity and for justice. (And, yes, it can be a tricky business, listening for and to such things. Among all the other ways listening can fail is a pull towards a flat listening, a consumptive extraction of these calls from the complex, messy, lived wholeness of which they are a part, which can be its own imposition of indignity and harm. I hope the following paragraphs do not replicate this, but perhaps they do.)

I hear someone I know, many someones I know, someone I just met down at the pub, someone I'm related to, someone across the table at an activist meeting. I hear them talk about working a lousy service-sector job to support their kids, to keep a roof overhead, to eat. I hear them talk about their day. It is totally ordinary — after all, making less than a living wage and having a lousy job and a horrible boss are utterly, completely, abysmally ordinary. So ordinary, in fact, that they often don't warrant a mention. They might just talk about the hilarious story that their co-worker told, because the not-enough-money, unpleasant-work, terrible-boss aspects of it are true every day, so why on earth say anything about them, and anyway he's not as bad as the last boss. Why talk about the toll it's taking on their body, the aches that no longer go away even with time off, not that there's ever much of that, and instead just grunt a bit when they sit. Or maybe these aspects are touched on with matter-of-factness, a shoulder shrug, "My dogs sure are barking today," all in a mode of complaint that itself doesn't convey the magnitude of it because it is so, so ordinary. "Shirley didn't show so I had to cover two sections, and my back is killing me." "Yeah, I only got two shifts next week. No idea how I'm going to make rent." "He called me 'exotic' and patted my ass again today. I swear, if I didn't need this job, I'd deck the fucker." "I was coughing up a lung, but they said they'd fire me if I missed another shift, so…"

I hear someone I know, many someones. I hear so many stories from so many women over so many years — wry or enraged or matter of fact or tired. Almost every woman I know well enough to know this kind of thing about has experienced gendered and/or sexual violence from a man at least once. I hear it because you can't swing a second-hand Simone de Beauvoir book without hitting accounts of how awful men can be — online, in person, to partners, to random women on the street, to Black women, to journalists, to actors, to trans women, to sex workers, to the many women who are more than one of those things. No, not all men, not all the time, but enough men, enough of the time. And all women. If men have real conversations with women, if they pay attention when women share their everyday lives on social media, if they read books written by women, they cannot avoid this. Oh, it is tempting to avoid it, because what if, at some point, many years ago, or yesterday, or every day, the source of harm was you, and you somehow manage to pretend you don't know? And yes, yes, it's not just men that deny this reality — some women do too. Women can also be awful, can also act to blatantly reproduce and enforce systemic indignity and harm along so many different axes. But how on earth is that enough to stop you from hearing the awfulness men do to women? It takes tremendous work to not hear it, active dismissal, a resolute and reflexive reading of earnest accounts of experience into not mattering, into irrelevance, into suspicion, into intellectualized debate that erases the fundamental humanity of those being harmed, into just not caring.

I hear someone I know, many someones — someone venting on social media, someone grumbling over lunch, someone sitting across a campfire, someone speaking strongly in meetings that don't want to hear them. I hear impassioned poems and countless news reports and books and books and books in every genre and form. I hear, again, complex, messy wholeness, full of joy and brilliance and thriving. But also stories of being followed in stores, being repeatedly stopped by police, having Children's Aid called when a white kid would be left to merrily go on their way, being mistaken for that other well-known Black man working in the same field in the same city by a potential employer who absolutely should know better. I hear exasperation at uninvited hair touching, pain at non-Black colleagues being oblivious to the impacts of that day's big news story, weary resignation at being read yet again into "angry" and "criminal." I hear a friend's utter exhaustion and fear for her sons. I hear words in many different modes and tones, of course, but sometimes a distinctive mix of the resolute and the very, very careful that speaks to the daily impossible pressure to balance the absolute necessity and the entirely predictable consequences of speaking up — as Black studies professor Christina Sharpe puts it, "Speech and speechlessness; each one has a cost."[9]

I hear someone I know, an old friend. We talk about our respective families, work, summer plans, dreams. We catch each other up about people we both know and about loved ones in our lives that the other has never met. It is ordinary, wonderful, rich, full. Plenty of joy, plenty of humour, plenty of life-well-lived, with the smooch-hello, moving-into-a-new-place, going-to-visit-a-parent, new-family-baby, travel-dreams, work-gossip of life. But also, the tentacles in her family and immediate community of so much intergenerational colonial trauma are there, plainly and clearly. Both of us speak of addiction and trauma and street involvement and mental illness and gendered harm in our families, but the differences in how they play out, in what they carry with them, are so, so stark.

Listening to the *more* carried by the words of the people in our lives is central to engaging with their full complexity and richness. If we took in only the words of others, only the surface level of their emanations, we would miss a great deal of what makes them *them*. Whatever we might build together on that basis would, I think, be much less robust, much less meaningful. As with the beep, though, and with my friend's passing mention of her experiences of street harassment, the substance of that *more* carried by the words of the people in our lives *always* echoes down the social relations preceding and surrounding them. Whether we pay sufficient attention to them or not, we are always listening, in an imperfect and fragmentary way, to the aspects of the social world that made them, that matter to them. We are, as we listen, learning about the world around them, about how it appears through the lens of their standpoint, about the analyses and narratives they've developed to understand it. This means that we are not just learning about something that is individual to them — we are learning about the world, full stop, from a vantage that differs from our own, that reveals different things, that perhaps challenges what we thought we knew.

Though you can engage with this *more* in an intellectualized way, it is often experienced as a feeling, a sense, an impression. It is not the knowledge of rigorous investigation, and any one instance can be vague and unsure. It is never the same as knowing the social world through your own experience or as them knowing the world through theirs. Yet it accumulates. It sediments. It interacts with what you already know and feel, with shapes cast into your mind on previous occasions by this person and at other times by other people. It becomes, over time, more solid, more sure.

The world you glimpse through this *more* is the same world you listen to from where *you* are, the same world that made both them and you. Figuring out how to build a useful whole from the many pieces, from the many standpoints you encounter in such fleeting ways as you move through your days — figuring out how to connect them, how to integrate them — often requires moving from everyday conversation to other resources for learning. This can be where theory and rigorous investigation are crucial tools for coming to understand why the world does this to me and that to you, X over here and Y over there, and how these things are not just different but connected and emerging differentially from a common source for concrete, material reasons. Yet even just with conversation, over time, you have the possibility of gradually, partially, sometimes only vaguely, but potentially in a deeply body- and feeling-integrated way, piecing together knowledge about the social world beyond your own life but deeply relevant to it. It provides you with opportunities for developing a better understanding of how you and the person you are listening to are connected, how both of you are connected to that person over there and how, to put it simplistically, the world works. Moreover, if you are listening deeply and well, because you are learning things about the world that shaped you but from standpoints other than your own, your understanding of yourself will be gradually transformed as well.

chapter five

failures and harms

Listening is not always effective — not mine, not yours, not anyone's. Sometimes, we attempt to take in, take up, and make meaning from the sensory landscape in which we are embedded and from the voices of those with whom we are in relation, and we get it wrong. All of us know this. It is, after all, just part of life, though that knowledge doesn't make it any less distressing or difficult to deal with. We don't necessarily give much thought, however, to how these failures of listening happen, where they come from, and what that means. Perhaps even less appreciated is that when listening *is* effective, it is not always a good thing. Our culture tends to treat listening as only and inherently positive, but listening is just as bound up with causing harm and propagating injustice as it is with the opposite. Neither of these things — listening that is ineffective, listening that is unjust — can be understood solely at the individual level any more than listening as a whole can. Both are bound up with how the social world is organized in ways that go far beyond what individuals, on our own, can do anything about.

listening is not enough

Let's start with me. Sometimes, as is true of all of us, listening fails me. Perhaps I cannot hear, or I do not notice, or I refuse to see, or I will not listen. Or the sound (sight, smell) passes me by, or I filter it out, or it means nothing to me, so it gets tossed in the bin labelled "noise." Or I do sense it, I take it in and take it up, but the knowledge I make mismatches the world.

Part of it can be physical. I remember an instance when I was 12 and another when I was 38 that were catastrophic (or so it felt) and humiliating (or so it felt) failures of listening which in part were about the physical environment. In both cases it was loud and chaotic, and that made it hard to understand speech. Except the problem was not just the physical environment. It was also the social environment and me in that social environment. In both cases, I was anxious. In both cases, the intensity of my anxiety was like static interfering with my listening, a kind of competing signal or internal noise that disrupted my ability to hear and that wrought havoc with my machinery for taking up and making meaning.

In the earlier instance, the Grade 8 class at my small rural elementary school had been invited to a dance by the more numerous and (to my mind) more sophisticated students of the same grade in a city school, because we would all be going together on a multi-day field trip later in the year. At the dance, a girl I didn't recognize came up to me and started talking as if she knew me. I couldn't really tell what she was saying and had no idea who she was. She soon left, looking less than thrilled with the interaction. Only much later did I realize she was someone I had known from a program I had been in the year before — looking very different fancied up for the dance, in a context where I had no idea to expect her, in loud noise and poor light, while I was practically vibrating with the anxiety I felt at *any* dance in those years, let alone one filled with strangers. She was also someone I not only had known but had gotten along with well and really liked. After my no doubt humiliating-to-her response, she made no further attempts to interact with me at the dance or later on the trip, and I was so ashamed once I realized what had happened that I didn't make any attempt to interact with her either.[1]

The instance in my 30s was a labour-related gathering in Toronto. I had been invited by someone I had interviewed and had also worked with briefly on a project years before to be present with my then-new books on social movement history before the event. At a certain point, two older white women approached, and we chatted a little. It was almost time for the event to start, so the venue was full and loud, and it was hard for me to hear. My anxiety was not as urgent as at the dance two and a half decades earlier, but with the necessity for self-promotion and schmoozing with strangers, it was definitely present. Still, I managed to give the obligatory answers to the predictable questions about my books. Then one of them started to tell me about … something. After asking her to repeat herself twice, I made some response I immediately knew made it clear I still hadn't understood what she was saying. Then the interaction ended (with some evidence of exasperation on her part), and it clicked for me. I had managed to fight through anxiety and noise to answer questions about *my* work, but when it was two older working-class women talking about leading a community-based labour history project, somehow my brain could not make the connection.

Failures of listening in specific moments — failures easily attributable at least in part to external interference (like noise) or internal interference (like anxiety) — are often easy to identify as we experience them. But even without examining it more closely, it seems clear that in my second example there was something else going on as well.

harm shapes our listening

Many of the ways listening can fail are socially produced. We talked earlier about the fact that because we learn to listen by listening, our listening practices themselves are shaped by our experience of the world. Hegemonic ideas and stories shape everyone's listening practices, albeit not all in the same ways, and can result in all sorts of mismatches between the world and what we come to know through listening. Moreover, my life and your life are socially organized into different experiences of the world, notably including the fact that we face different trajectories of socially produced benefit and harm,[2] so we develop different ranges of listening practices that are more or less effective and more or less likely to be part of propagating indignity, harm, and injustice in those areas.

A concrete example might help illustrate what I mean. There is a lot more nuance and complexity to it than this, but at its bluntest, if you get harmed by a given axis of power — I'll use racism as the example in the next few paragraphs, but it applies in not identical but analogous ways to other axes — then the impulse to avoid harm nudges you towards paying certain kinds of attention to it and developing certain kinds of listening practices that can detect, anticipate, and mitigate it. At least with racism, there is additionally a good chance that you grew up in a local environment surrounded by adults who already know and talk about such things, and their accounts of the world were also part of what shaped you.

On the other hand, if you benefit from racism, then not only is there an absence of that kind of incentive to pay attention to it and to develop practices of listening and knowing related to it, but there is an incentive to *not* pay attention, to not know.[3] White people are much less likely to develop listening practices — from noticing on up through all of the things we do to make meaning — that can adequately deal with racism and white supremacy. This is not simply a matter of accidental not-knowing. It is not, in contrast with how some people deploy it, a ready-made excuse to deflect political accountability. For one thing, as rudimentary as white people's capacities to listen and know can be when it comes to racism, I think we are often far more aware of it than we admit. But beyond that, part of growing up benefiting from systemic violence and harm and part of the incentive to not pay attention, to not know, can include a visceral and libidinal investment in the status quo that benefits us and in avoiding anything that might threaten our ability to believe in our own goodness, deservingness, even superiority. There is also often a similar investment in maintaining a worldview that denigrates or devalues people who face racist harms — whether that is an open, hood-wearing, swastika-brandishing investment, or the much more common quiet, smug, denying-it-even-to-self liberal one — and a refusal to treat their suffering as fully valid or meaningful.

Of course, unlike how this is sometimes represented in popular discourse, it is not some reified, schematic thing in which "if you are X, that automatically means Y." Black, Indigenous, and other racialized people have vast, diverse spectrums of analysis, politics, practices of listening and knowing and ways of moving through the world with respect to racism. While experiencing harm incentivizes paying attention and developing knowledge that might reduce its impacts, it is no guarantee of specific outcomes. This is further complicated by the fact that while there are endless variations and nuances, most hegemonic stories of the world push people to listen to their experiences of harm in ways that obfuscate, confuse, and encourage self-blame and self-hate.[4] As queer African American sociologist and scholar of racism Crystal Fleming observes, "One of the main consequences of centuries of racism is that we are all systematically exposed to racial stupidity and racist beliefs that warp our understandings of society, history, and ourselves"[5] and "nonwhites are, unfortunately, not immune to absorbing and disseminating distortions of racial reality."[6] As well, pressure to pay certain kinds of attention is no guarantee of having access to the knowledge beyond experience that might put it in a broader context. Renowned African American feminist bell hooks wrote, "Simply being the victim of an exploitative or oppressive system and even resisting it does not mean we understand why it's in place or how to change it."[7] US-based Menominee abolitionist organizer Kelly Hayes puts it this way:

> Experiencing violence doesn't necessarily give us an analysis of that violence, or a sense of strategy for confronting that violence. Experience can be valuable when forming an analysis, but if trauma, by itself, gave us the political calculus that we needed to get free, we would have gotten free generations ago.[8]

There is, of course, breadth among white people too — including, for some, varying kinds and levels of anti-racist commitment and related practices of listening and knowing.

Even with all those caveats, however, our different experiences of oppression and privilege play a central role in shaping our listening practices at every step along the way. They do not mandate it in an absolute sense — as Fleming says, "these dynamics are *probabilistic* rather than *deterministic*"[9] — but the incentives to know and to not-know, to be invested in not being harmed or in continuing to benefit, are still powerful. This is, perhaps, most obvious at the more cognitive end of the spectrum of things that we do to listen, from the specifics of the schemas and scripts we develop to the content of the pool of knowledge we accumulate over time, with their central roles in how we take up and assess new knowledge.

It is a lot more than just that, though. For one thing, the visceral attachment we develop to a status quo that benefits us can powerfully reinforce our commitment to our existing listening practices, even at that more cognitive level. But our listening practices themselves also involve lots of gut-level elements that are formed in and reproduce these oppressive social relations. Think back, for example, to our sense of out-of-placeness. It is about lots more than how we react to nighttime noises. Most of us, through our listening to the world and to the dominant stories that surround us, also develop a sense of some *people* as being out of place in some contexts, so we notice them more and differently. That might go along with us having some explicit objection to their presence in those contexts, but it often does not — either way, it means they are subjected to greater scrutiny just because of who they are. Greater scrutiny can be one element of the oppressive experiences faced by, say, the only woman in some rarefied room where power is exercised or in some masculine-coded workplace, and of the constant surveillance in all kinds of spaces that is so central to Black experience in Canada,[10] and, in a different way, to the experiences of many trans women.[11] Out-of-placeness is just one example. There are lots of ways that we are hardly aware of that an oppressive world shapes our feelings, our gut reactions, our instincts, and the many related doings that are involved in listening.

Much of the listening we do that might reveal systemic violence and harm, and assertions of dignity and resistance, comes to us via the ordinary, everyday sights and sounds that are the murmur. Particularly if we have grown up believing that things are fine as they are (or mostly fine), if we think there is no other way for things to be, or if our sense of self and stability and what makes us worthy are premised on a status quo that just happens to benefit us, then we easily allow ourselves to be lulled by all the other moments in the soundtrack of everyday life into not noticing the moments of harm, violence, and resistance that pervade it. Evidence of people's capacity to *persist, despite* — to find joy and to get on with things, to make the best of it, to create beauty amidst pain, to be "resilient" (to borrow a piece of neoliberal jargon), to make dumb jokes even while life is awful — is mobilized to avoid taking seriously or even really noticing how systemic violence and harm, and resistance to them, are nonetheless there. The murmur soothes, calms, distracts, and often we want it to. The common sense of the world built from such refusal to listen then makes it all the easier when the violence is named directly and explicitly, when the scream breaks through, for us to hold on to our denial, to scoff — to say, no, that cannot be, life is not like that, no.

In my example in the previous section from the labour event, even though if you asked me I would oppose any suggestion that movement history work or intellectual work in general are the province of middle-class white guys, I suspect that some classist and/or sexist construction buried in my existing knowledge contributed to my inability to push through the environmental interference and into comprehension. "Hey, we do work like you," clearly wasn't a possibility close enough to the surface of my consciousness for me to fight through the static and grab on to it. There are many other kinds of scenarios as well where listening practices that have been shaped in experiences of benefit from the status quo fail, in one way or another. For instance, I entered university with little understanding beyond shallow liberal platitudes of what it might mean to listen effectively to talk of race and racism, and as a consequence I know, in retrospect, I caused little indignities and harms in that first year. I remember how, at the same age, gender privilege and shame (itself a product of my experiences of both privilege and harm in the context of social relations related to gender and sexuality) had stunted my capacity to comprehend talk of sexuality and desire — mine or anyone else's, though particularly women's — in complex, grounded, critical ways. I like to think I had good intentions and good will in both of those areas, but those are seldom enough. So, our listening is more likely to fail us in relation to axes of the social world where we experience benefit.[12] There can be lots of nuance to this, lots of complexity, but broadly speaking, this is the case.

listening and harm

Listening that is in some sense ineffective is not the only way that listening can fail. A pervasive assumption that underlies almost all the mainstream sources about listening that I touched on earlier in the book is that listening is only and inherently a good thing. What kind of good thing varies — maybe it is good because it is practically useful for achieving our goals, maybe it is good because it is virtuous, maybe it is good because it will lead to happiness and well-being or even to a better world. But good, we are told, listening most definitely is. This is, of course, not entirely false. After all, it is pretty easy to look at our own experience and find many circumstances in which listening is a positive thing. When people in your life listen to you (and vice versa), it strengthens your relationships, it enables collaborative activities, it helps you know things, and so on — and, often, it just feels better than not being listened to. Even though we are seldom perfect in how we go about it, most of us instinctively know that listening well to those around us is the right thing to be doing.

At the same time, there are lots of situations where listening plays a much less positive role. A very ordinary example: When I was in high school, I played on the school basketball team. One summer, one or two of my teammates and I went to a week-long basketball camp in upstate New York. I was trying to fall asleep one night when I heard voices percolating through an air vent from the next room, including one I recognized as belonging to a guy I had been getting to know a little bit. They were talking about the players at the camp. I don't remember this erstwhile potential camp friend being particularly mean about it, but there is a certain ruthlessness to how many young men in sports judge each other, and his assessment of my modest skills was accurate but not gentle. He also seemed to think I was a nice enough fellow but — well, I don't remember what teenage euphemism for "socially awkward" he used, but something to that effect. He was not saying anything I did not already know about myself — there was no silver lining in the form of insight from this accidental listening. It just sucked. Describing it as "traumatizing" would be putting it much too strongly, but it didn't make me feel very good, and I obviously still remember it three decades later.

However you might categorize this experience, it shows one way that listening can be a not-so-good thing — listening can, itself, be a way that you experience what in my case was unpleasantness, and in others can legitimately be understood as indignity or suffering, or even harm. In recent decades, the language of "microaggressions"[13] has been used to talk about how oppressive social relations get expressed and reproduced in the context of everyday interactions. Any individual instance might (especially to someone not on the receiving end of the oppression in question) seem to be small and unimportant but, particularly cumulatively, they can cause significant indignity, suffering, and harm. For much of this painful everyday-level racism, sexism, ableism, homophobia, and so on, listening is how it lands — you read the email, you hear the comment, etc. There are ways listening is a mechanism of suffering and harm beyond the micro, too. Take a household where the father is emotionally abusive, where he targets some members of the family with verbal denigration and humiliation, forcing both them and everyone else in the family to listen, thereby causing harm of various sorts to everyone involved. As well, it's not unusual for physical violence targeting people who are oppressed to be accompanied by verbal abuse that communicates that targeting and adds an additional layer of harm. There is even the use the US military and other oppressive institutions make of sensory interventions like around-the-clock bright lights or "torture by music," in which extremely loud rock music is played incessantly at captives as part of breaking them.[14] In these situations, suffering and harm happen at least in part through listening.

Far more common than listening as a direct mechanism of harm are instances where other kinds of harm are enabled through listening. Listening, after all, is how we know whatever we know about the world, it informs our decisions, it shapes our actions — and that is no less true of actions that reproduce oppression and cause harm. Across the entire scale through which oppressive and harmful experiences are forced into people's lives, from the most fleeting microaggression to the all-encompassing systemic violences that shape the world, listening is part of the mechanism, the *how*.

Even though listening is integral both to things we would say are good and things we would say are bad, harmful, or oppressive, our culture associates the former with listening but is much less likely to do so with the latter. So, at least for me, the careful listening that is part of building connection and intimacy with another person just *feels* like it is centrally about the listening, like it is somehow inherent to what listening is and what listening does in our lives. When someone is described as a "good listener," that's generally what people mean. On the other hand, when I think about the careful listening that is part of manipulating and abusing someone, it doesn't feel like that harm is centrally about the listening, despite how essential the listening is to the harm. Nobody would look at a situation like that and say, "Wow, he sure is a good listener," no matter how central his skill at observation is to the power he exerts over his partner. I think, however, if we want to have a richer understanding of listening, one thing we need to do is let go of this tendency to associate listening only with its positive uses.

Some popular sources hint at this ambivalent character of listening without intending to do so. Some take an instrumental approach to listening, at least in part, and emphasize its role in you getting what you want.[15] They still construct listening as a good thing and suggest that it is precisely because it is useful in accomplishing your goals that it is good, but I found it quite difficult to read those sources without imagining the various unsavoury characters I have met over my life who so obviously relate to the people around them in ways that are primarily about their own benefit. You can go beyond the sources I survey to things like the range of popular misogyny in books and websites that aim to help young men become so-called "pick-up artists." For all their dehumanization of women, such sources do counsel that men engage in a particular kind of listening to the women they want to have sex with — it just happens to be an instrumental kind of listening and one that makes the role listening can play in manipulating and exerting power over someone else obvious.

While writing this book, I kept running into another peculiar manifestation of how strong the cultural pressure is for us to perceive listening as only and always good. Consider the long list of people who have done or supported terrible things and who have also had positive things to say about listening. Take Donald Rumsfeld, who among other positions over many years, served as the secretary of defence for US President George W. Bush between 2001 and 2006. In that capacity, he was centrally involved in the US invasion of Afghanistan and Iraq and other war-making in western Asia and beyond, at the expense of tens of thousands of US lives and millions of civilian lives in the targeted countries. In his book *Rumsfeld's Rules,* which contains his decades of accumulated wisdom for success in government and in life, he offers this rule (which he sources to a Dr. R. Barr of St. John's College): "The art of listening is indispensable for the right use of the mind. It is also the most gracious, the most open, and the most generous of human habits."[16]

Mark Goulston's *Just Listen: Discover the Secret to Getting Through to Absolutely Anyone* quotes John Marhsall, the chief justice of the US Supreme Court between 1801 and 1835: "To listen well is as powerful a means of communication and influence as to talk well."[17] Marshall wrote for the majority in the decision that ensrhined in US law the Doctrine of Discovery, whereby European nations claimed sovereignty on non-European lands just by planting a flag — one of the legal pillars of settler colonialism in the United States.[18]

Rebecca Shafir in *The Zen of Listening* favourably cites famous twentieth-century US-based white evangelical Christian leader Rev. Billy Graham on the importance of listening,[19] with no consideration of his horrific statements on homosexuality or his ardent support for the Vietnam War, which killed millions of civilians.[20] Shafir also quotes Sam Walton, founder of the Walmart dynasty: "The key to success is to get out into the store and listen to what the associates have to say. It's terribly important for everyone to get involved. Our best ideas come from clerks and stock boys."[21] There is, of course, no shortage of articles and books documenting the harm that Walmart has done to workers and communities.[22]

In thinking about how most of us are likely to read these quotes, as well as about the decisions by authors of books about listening to cite some of these people, it is clear that we are deeply trained not to make any connection between listening and the terrible things that these people have done or supported. At most, we might snort at the hypocrisy of Rumsfeld or Walton for endorsing listening while clearly not doing it well or often enough. Probably, we read the quote in question, agree with it in a vague way, and go about our business. We are unlikely to recognize the ways these quotes call for a more profound questioning of listening's role in the world, because we are trained to miss how listening is inevitably a mechanism in whatever awfulness these people have perpetrated and endorsed.

The point of noting this is not to enact some cheap "gotcha" on authors who cite particular people as authorities on listening. I mean, look at me — one of the books I quietly referenced in Chapter 2 is *The Lost Art of Good Conversation: A Mindful Way to Connect with Others and Enrich Everyday Life* by Sakyong Mipham, the head of the Shambhala tradition of Tibetan Buddhism. I am not sure if the allegations of sexual misconduct, abuse, and assault against him had not yet broken when I first read it, or if I, as someone not part of that community, was just unaware of them.[23] Nonetheless, as I read his book, it did not occur to me even once to wonder if this spiritual leader might have deployed his listening skills in harmful ways.

listening's failures and harms are socially produced

If we pay attention to the ways our listening can be ineffective and unjust, there is, in part thanks to the strong pressure to regard listening as a purely individual phenomenon, a pull towards responses that are just as individualist. There is a temptation to turn the bulk of my attention to figuring out how to listen better, how to do it such that it fails me less often and less severely. I feel an impulse to become a better self, that oh so neoliberal compulsion that echoes a much older vocabulary of sin and virtue. Improve, we are told. Develop your skills, your capacities, your practices. Make yourself a better person and listen better by sheer force of will. Our capacities to listen can and do shift as we go through life, of course. Listening can indeed sediment over time into practices that lead to better listening, though it is by no means guaranteed to do so, and work in that direction at an individual level is not just possible but is, to a certain extent, a political responsibility. But the barriers to listening effectively and justly transcend individual frailty or failure — they are baked deeply into how the world is socially organized.

It is worth sitting for a bit with the magnitude and the sheer inertia of socially produced ineffective and harmful listening. Take my understanding of what I have heard over the years from many people who have devoted their lives to grassroots political work in opposition to one or many axes of oppression along which I experience benefit. That group is nowhere near to being a monolith — no group is — but my understanding of what I have most often heard is that individual work by people who benefit can on the one hand be useful for making spaces more liveable and reducing, to an extent, certain kinds of interpersonal indignity and harm. On the other, it is unwise to invest undue hope in what can be achieved, either individually or cumulatively, through trying to persuade individual oppressors to change their conduct. Whatever else is needed, whatever else is possible, pushing those of us who benefit from and are often invested in a harmful status quo towards better behaviour, towards better listening, towards being better selves, is not enough — it is not, I would argue, even close to enough.

Even aside from that, though, we live in a world that is continually producing and reproducing circumstances in which listening is likely to fail. We live in a world that continues, moreover, to produce *listeners* whose listening is likely to fail and who are often actively committed to listening that fails in terms of both effectiveness and justice. Of *course* prodding and pushing and cajoling individuals to change while the circumstances which are socially producing all that chug along unaltered, or at best slightly mitigated, is just not going to be sufficient.

To really bring this point home, I want to look in a little more detail at what some of the sharpest minds of the last half century have had to say about one particular axis of power. Colonialism — including the form through which European nations preyed upon what we now think of as the Global South, the settler colonialism through which European-derived societies have come to dominate Turtle Island and other non-European places, and the enslavement of African-descended people — has been central to shaping the world we live in. Palestinian American activist and scholar Edward Said's *Orientalism*[24] and Maori scholar Linda Tuhiwai Smith's *Decolonizing Methodologies*[25] explore how colonialism has shaped the ways in which we know the world — the ways in which, to put it in the language I am using in this book, we are able to listen. Said's book looks at how ways of knowing took shape as part of Western projects of colonial domination of what often gets called the "Middle East" but points to related dynamics in other parts of the world as well. Smith's book is a landmark in efforts by Indigenous Peoples from around the world to engage in research that centres their own needs, their own practices, and their own knowledge systems, and it includes an overview of histories of Western knowledge production, research, and scholarship.

These works (and many others on this topic) have different focuses and approaches but paint a broadly consistent picture. They both illustrate how, in Smith's words, in Western contexts "the pursuit of knowledge is deeply embedded in the multiple layers of imperial and colonial practice."[26] And they both talk about how those ways of knowing and the knowledge they produce have been integral to the processes of colonial and imperial domination. What the colonizer comes to know usually has a tenuous relationship at best to the actual real lives and experiences of those being studied. Rather, it is more about representing them in ways that are comforting and useful to those listening and knowing and in particular is a knowing that is organized around extracting value from the lands and peoples that are colonized and enabling the colonizer to rule. This is not just some curiosity of the past but has persisted over time, constantly reinvented across generations. As Smith writes, "Research within late-modern and late-colonial conditions continues relentlessly and brings with it a new wave of exploration, discovery, exploitation and appropriation."[27] And it is not just part of formal efforts to learn about colonized peoples and about the world but pervades all manner of informal knowledge production as well — travellers' tales, journalism, fiction, and the like. Said talks about how practices with origins in earlier moments of colonial domination seep into all manner of knowledge and representation today — Arabs are this, Muslims are that, these countries are inherently whatever else, as seen in fiction, film, news reporting, and scholarship.

One aspect of these dominating ways of knowing, observable in everything from the most crudely racist research of centuries past to the behaviour of many well-intentioned white progressives on social media today, is relating to Indigenous Peoples and other Others as objects while trying to listen to and know about them. As Smith points out, "Objectification is a process of dehumanization."[28] She elaborates: "Imperialism provided the means through which concepts of what counts as human could be applied systematically as forms of classification, for example through hierarchies of race and typologies of different societies."²⁹ In other words, explicitly or implicitly treating certain people as not human or as less human is integral to colonial/imperial ways of knowing the world and colonial/imperial ways of organizing the world, and this is what comes down to us in a million different ways as the racist devaluation, degradation, and dismissal of colonized and racialized peoples today. As Black Canadian writer and organizer Robyn Maynard writes, this "violent *ejection* of some, most, of the world's inhabitants from the conception of who is considered to be human"³⁰ in the course of the Industrial Revolution was in the service of "building a white (settler) vision of a future society in which [Black and Indigenous] peoples' respective survival was an afterthought,"³¹ and this continues to inform mainstream understandings of the world today.

Radical Jamaican intellectual Sylvia Wynter has thoroughly explored how inclusions and expulsions from what counts as "human" have shaped the world.³² She writes about the idea of genres of the human produced through social mechanisms in a way that writes deeply on not just the social world but on our very selves and bodies. Much of the last five centuries can be understood as a single genre of the human — the straight, white, bourgeois, Euro-American man, which she describes as Man, though there's more to it than this — coming to dominate the world both materially and also in terms of seizing exclusive definition of what it means to be human, and becoming, in Katherine McKittrick's words, "the measuring stick through which all other forms of being are measured."³³ Some people are expelled completely from the human thus defined; some are understood as human, but provisionally so, marginally so, less so.

Moreover, this approach to organizing and knowing the world has expanded to become part of how social power works along its many axes. McKittrick writes: "Our present analytic categories — race, class, gender, sexuality, margins and centers, insides and outsides — tell a partial story, wherein humanness continues to be understood in hierarchical terms."³⁴ She continues: "Powerful knowledge systems and origin stories … produce the lived and racialized categories" that are so deeply constitutive of our social world, but they also "signal the processes through which the empirical and experiential lives of *all* humans are increasingly subordinated to a figure [i.e., Man] that thrives on accumulation."³⁵ The ways of knowing and ways of listening that are most readily available to us are shaped by all this, including what and who is valued, and how all of us and the world are understood. Such knowing is inadequate to the dignity and humanity of those expelled wholly or partly from the category of "human," and they are part of how that expulsion is continually reproduced. Though the impact on us varies tremendously, all of us come to be in the context of these dominant, dehumanizing ways of organizing the world and of organizing listening and knowing.

A core logic in our inherited colonial practices of listening and knowing is a relentless drive to what Martinican writer Édouard Glissant names "transparency."[36] This is listening and knowing that presume no barriers and a right to access everything and everyone. It is a measuring, a comparing, a judging, a reducing, a categorizing that is imposed as part of domination. It is listening and knowing directed towards elements of nature to be turned into commodities in the service of profit and towards people assumed to be Other and lesser, who perhaps possess (or will be treated as) resources the listener wants. It is knowing on the knower's terms, in the knower's categories, where knowing is often *done to* rather than consensual. It is the assumption that this is just how you relate to the world, that this is the only way listening and knowing can happen — at least for you and for people like you. This drive underlies the objectifying colonial scrutiny that Said and Smith wrote about, the "hungry listening" from a writer and scholar we will meet later,[37] bell hooks' "eating the Other,"[38] and analogous phenomena described by so many other authors. It is listening and knowing that consume, that are predatory, that fix people in categories that imprison and limit while centring the needs and desires of the listener, the knower. From scholarship to popular media, to so much of how liberal-minded, privileged people in the West relate to difference, this drive to transparency can be just as powerful today as when Glissant was writing. You could probably even make a case that it has intensified because of the ways in which social media has heightened expectations of being able to see, to listen, to know anything the person holding the smartphone desires.

thinking of power in terms of listening

In this chapter, I talk about how listening is not always effective, how it can sometimes be a direct mechanism of indignity and harm, and how it is central in a broader sense to enabling indignity and harm. Moreover, none of this can be reduced to the level of individuals. There are some ways in which absolute physical limitations and basic human frailty can be part of how listening is ineffective or unjust, but there is also a significant extent to which these things are a product of how our social world is organized. Listening is part of how indignity and harm, oppression and injustice, happen because listening is part of how everything happens.

It is possible to extend this a little bit. Because of the integral role of listening in how the world works, including how socially organized oppressive power works, we can use listening as a lens for thinking and talking about power. We can use it as a way to frame oppression and exploitation on the one hand and resistance to those things on the other. This person, this institution, this set of relations is harming us, and we do not wish to be harmed. We have never wished to be harmed, we have signalled that repeatedly. But the person, the institution, the overall circumstance is not listening to us, not being responsive. Moreover, the situation is such that they are *able* to not listen to us. This capacity to not listen to those whom you are harming is a key aspect of having power over. In the spirit of how we have been talking about listening, this is not necessarily about an individual making a deliberate choice (though it can be) — the lack of listening, the lack of responsiveness, the capacity to not be responsive are a product of how the situation is socially organized, and changing that is central to making things better.

It goes beyond that, though. Yes, some subset of people is not being listened to, but other groups — more powerful groups — are being listened to instead. Some people's needs, voices, and humanity are not heard, while others' are not only heard but revered and responded to far beyond what justice would warrant. It is not just about the presence or absence of listening, though. It is also about its character. Perhaps this person, this institution, this set of relations is listening (responsive) to oppressed people, but this listening is surveillance, consumption, predation. It is listening done as part of enacting oppression, indignity, and harm. It is the social assistance system not only refusing to be responsive to the needs and voices and humanity of recipients beyond a bare minimum but also the way it is designed to be responsive to the needs of the rich (i.e., those who own capital) and how it devotes massive resources to forms of listening that surveil and police recipients.[39]

Those in the thick of the many struggles that shape our world say, we who are not listened to in the contexts that shape our lives must be heard. We must, by building power among those whose struggles overlap with ours (and those whose do not), make institutions and relations that constrain us, that hurt us, that limit our possibilities for thriving, fully responsive to our needs, our voices, our humanity. We must, moreover, make a world that is less responsive to our oppressors, that does not listen to their every whim and cater to their every demand — we want *less* listening to those who push an agenda of injustice. We must end the listening that surveils us, that allows oppressive institutions to prey upon us and take our lives and our joy. We want new modes of listening that give us the power we need to shape the circumstances of our lives, new social forms that listen in ways that enact reciprocity, respect, dignity, consent, and care for everyone. We seek to have the decision changed, to change who makes the decision, to change the social relations that produced the indignity and harm to begin with.

It is not clear to me that we gain a whole lot from this lens, this re-framing, at least on its own. After all, we already have plenty of ways to talk about the social world and about injustice and struggle. But the fact that we can think about oppression and resistance in terms of listening in a big-picture way suggests that we could also think, with listening in mind, about the nuts and bolts of how people act, on our own and together, as we navigate the oppression in our lives and as we come together to resist collectively. This, I think, might be rather more useful.

part 3

listening and change

chapter six

everyday resistance

Most of us, most of the time, are just trying to live our lives. We are eating, sleeping, loving the people we love, doing the things we do, having a little fun when we can, and moving forward to the best of our ability. As we have seen, all this is in the context of a world that is socially organized in highly uneven and profoundly unjust ways.

I could talk about this injustice in terms of the life- and world-pervading figures of the scream and the murmur, but to stick more tightly to the level of everyday experience, it might be useful to approach it instead through thinking about concrete, lived moments. In some moments, people face denials of dignity, harm, someone taking, someone doing to, you can't, you must, you aren't, you don't belong, you can only be, you aren't fully human. Such moments happen all the time, everywhere, but distributed in a grossly unequal way. And they are not just one thing. They can be direct violence, loss of life. They can be sharp and sudden, an abrupt intrusion, a breathtaking pain. They can be recurrent, predictable, a wearying drip, a re-battered bruise, an ongoing deprivation, a product of enduring relations that hurt and harm and take. They can be so ordinary, so ubiquitous, so built into how particular lives are socially organized that there is no clear singular moment to feel, just an every-moment presence. Or they can be something else entirely — this scattering of examples by no means exhausts the forms that they take. It is in and through those moments that we experience indignity and harm, and it is in and after them that we must do whatever we are going to do to navigate them.

In the next chapter, I talk about some of the big, visible, collective ways in which people sometimes take action to make change. But none of those would exist — none would need to exist — if it were not for the pervasive presence of these moments of indignity and harm experienced by so many people in the course of everyday life. So, in this chapter, I focus on how people exist in relation to those moments and on how people respond to them.

Before diving into the details, I want to emphasize two points. The first is that listening is just as central to how we respond to those moments as it is to any other facet of life. Something bad happens to you — some indignity, some harm — and you take it in through whatever sensory pathways are relevant, you process those sensations and make meaning from them, and you do something. Or something happens not to you but to someone else, and you see it and hear it and act accordingly. As you do those things, the listening practices that you bring to bear are those that have been shaped in your experience of benefit and harm over time, which will feed into what you notice, what meaning you make, and what action you take. The second point is that these moments need to be understood in social ways. As we have seen, whatever else we can say about the social world, it is not only unjust but also organized and interconnected. Any individual moment is not isolated but rather is a product of other moments, of people's practices, and of the socially organized relations among us. I focus below on discrete fragments of experience and on how we navigate them, but I try to do so in that social relational context rather than abstracted from it. Later in the chapter, I talk a bit more about some of the ways in which this matters.

orienting to moments

Some of the people who are *not* negatively impacted in a given moment of indignity and harm are the people who are active in creating the harm. Think of the person who utters the slur, the employer who decides not to hire because "they just wouldn't fit in," the person who writes the policy that makes it possible for the employer to do that, the man who touches without consent, the other man who does not believe the first one touched without consent, the lawyer who applies for the injunction against the land defenders and the judge who grants it, the legislator who votes to deprive low-wage workers of their rights or to ban drag shows, the cop who pulls the trigger. *Everyday participation* in indignity and harm, you might call this. Another layer of people are not actively doing things that make the harm happen but, like those who are, still passively benefit from it in some way. This is *everyday complicity* in indignity and harm — the default, passive relationship that comes with privilege. In practice, the distinction between complicity and active forms of causing harm can be hazy and may not always matter very much. As with the harm itself, complicity might be an acute moment, like hearing the Islamophobic encounter on the bus and turning away rather than seeking out a small way to support the hijabi woman being targeted. Or it might be less palpable and more systemic. At this moment, as I lie on my bed typing, there are any number of ongoing harms in the city outside my door related to, for instance, race and class and colonization that I am complicit in and that I benefit from, that are produced by the same social relations that produce my whiteness and middle-classness.

Participation and complicity are not the only possibilities, of course — you can also respond with *everyday solidarity*. Perhaps you are, in general, subject to harm along the axis in question, but you just didn't happen to get targeted this time, and you find little ways to support those who were. Or perhaps you are starting from a place of complicity. Even in and after such a moment, it is possible to renounce the pretence at disconnection that so often sustains complicity, to push back against the desire we often feel in moments when we become aware of our complicity to do something that allows us to claim innocence or virtue and instead to take that complicity as a starting point, a way to orient action that points towards justice.[1]

When you are the one on the sharp end of indignity and harm and therefore forced by the actions of others to listen to those impacts, there is similarly a range of ways to act in and after such moments. There are lots of ways we could talk about that, but I group them into three broad categories — *everyday living, everyday compliance,* and *everyday resistance.*[2]

Everyday living means getting on with life during and after an experience of harm. It can mean taking care of self or others to deal with the impacts of the harm. It can mean some form of low-key escape or avoidance — talking to a friend, smoking a cigarette, checking out for a few hours and marathoning a favourite show. Often, it means getting on with whatever else you need to be doing — cooking dinner, ringing the next customer through, or wiping your toddler's nose, because that is what needs to be done. A lot of what people do looks like the murmur we talked about earlier — like dignity asserted despite its denial, like getting on with life because life needs to be gotten on with, like living the next moment because that moment follows this one, even in moments of and after harm. The key thing is that everyday living is about people following the logic of their own lives in what they do then and next.

Sometimes, in moments of indignity and harm, individual oppressors, institutions, or the relations that form the context are trying to compel a specific outcome, a specific behaviour from the impacted person. Sometimes, in assessing the situation and their options, people go along with that because not doing so would be worse. This is everyday compliance. It can be as broad and general as existing in some ongoing systemically oppressive circumstance — say, being a migrant worker deprived via legislation of rights that citizens take for granted — and just kind of going along with it, because you see no good outcome from making a fuss. It can be as tragically ordinary as staying silent in the face of a comment made in your school or workplace that dehumanizes you, because of the likely consequences of speaking up. Maybe it is obeying the cop when he issues arbitrary orders because of the implicit but oh-so-clear threat that he will escalate his violence if you do not. Or maybe after a strike has been lost and the union broken, it is workers going back for half the pay because what other choice do they have. Far too often, compliance can be a tactically insightful, self-preserving choice and at some moments can be the only conceivable path forward.

Sometimes, though, despite the obstacles, despite the risks, despite the overt and latent threats, despite all the good reasons to quietly accept that this is how things are, people find some way to resist at the level of everyday life. This orientation to oppressive circumstances is the focus of the rest of the chapter.

These three categories — everyday living, compliance, and resistance — are not nearly as distinct as they might seem. Sometimes, just getting on with life and asserting dignity despite its denial overlaps with compliance — sometimes, sadly, the logic of what you need to do in your own life fits with what the oppressor wants. Sometimes, either or both of those things can obscure the fact of current or intended resistance. In the words of a writer we meet more fully in the next section, "It is no simple matter to determine just where compliance ends and resistance begins, as the circumstances lead many … to clothe their resistance in the public language of conformity."[3]

I am not interested in judging people for how they navigate the indignity and harm they face. You shouldn't either, particularly when thinking about scenarios that you never face yourself. It is easy, especially for those of us who are relatively privileged, to relate to these choices in a harmful, moralistic way — for those of us with radical politics to simplistically invert oppressor morality and treat everyday resistance as virtuous, and everyday living and everyday compliance as not. This is destructive and oppressive and not at all a way to enact solidarity. The rest of this chapter is about everyday resistance, but that is not out of a desire to treat it as morally superior to the other ways that people respond to indignity and harm. Rather, it is because I am working towards talking about more collective forms of struggle, and I think everyday resistance is an important but often neglected element of that conversation, as well as an important grounding for thinking through all manner of resistance and struggle in a way that pays attention to listening.

weapons of the weak

Everyday resistance involves experiencing some indignity or harm, acute or systemic; the inevitable listening through which you make meaning from that experience; and based on that listening, acting in the course of everyday life to resist. It is often not thought of as resistance by the person doing it or even thought of in political terms at all — it is just someone doing what they have to do in the moment. In this sense, it can overlap significantly with everyday living. It is speaking up despite the cost and the risk, because silence would be worse. It is seizing resources, space, or power, often (but not necessarily) covertly. It can be acting to support, care for, and nurture others who are also harmed. It is asserting dignity in the face of its denial.

In scholarly contexts, the recognition of these moments and their significance, and the use of the phrase "everyday resistance" in this way, is generally traced to a book called *Weapons of the Weak*, published in 1985 by James C. Scott, a political scientist with anarchist sympathies. The book reports on ethnographic field work Scott did studying class relations in a peasant village in Malaysia.[4]

You do not have to look far to find ideas that link resistance with everyday life and that value resistance *in* everyday life in earlier writers, particularly radicals. Scott himself points towards famous thinkers of resistance like writer George Orwell, English historian of working-class struggle E.P. Thompson, and revolutionary Rosa Luxemburg as understanding any resistance by the oppressed as grounded in experiences of indignity and harm in everyday life.[5] In his 1935 classic *Black Reconstruction in America,* radical African American writer and scholar W.E.B. Du Bois includes descriptions of what amounts to everyday resistance among slaves in the pre–Civil War United States.[6] Dutch council communist Anton Pannekoek wrote in the 1940s: "Every shop, every enterprise, even outside of times of sharp conflict, of strikes and wage reductions, is the scene of a constant silent war, of a perpetual struggle, of pressure and counter-pressure."[7] A small leftist group which included famous names like C.L.R. James and Grace Lee Boggs wrote in the late 1950s: "People all over the world, and particularly ordinary working people in factories, mines, fields, and offices, are rebelling every day in ways of their own invention," including sometimes "on a small personal scale."[8] Writing just a few years before Scott, well-known chroniclers of poor people's movements Francis Fox Piven and Richard Cloward admonished those who understand resistance by poor people only in terms of formal movements rather than as inclusive of the kinds of dispersed refusal and defiance that are ubiquitous in poor communities.[9] And of course you have the billions who themselves engage in these kinds of activities, entirely untroubled by whether left and scholarly understandings might see value in what they are doing.

Despite this recognition in some radical traditions, the orthodoxy against which Scott was writing in *Weapons of the Weak* was one that tended to cast peasants as passive in the face of their oppression. This is bound up in Marxist arguments about the social roles of different classes, particularly an influential strand of analysis that understands peasants as a class as passive (or reactionary, in moments) in contrast with the central revolutionary role attributed to industrial workers. But some argue that the implications of these politics extend beyond this, perhaps even to the point of implying that either ordinary people are not capable of listening to the circumstances in which they experience indignity and harm and responding meaningfully at the level of everyday life, or that they are but it is politically irrelevant.

As he built relationships with and listened carefully to the residents of the Malaysian village, Scott heard a great deal that convinced him that this was just flat-out wrong. The context was stratified by class, along the lines of whether someone owned land or not and how much.

It was a moment when social relations in this part of Malaysia were being transformed by the reorganization of agriculture along capitalist lines that was being imposed on the Global South as a whole. It did not take the form of open, collective defiance, but he found a lively class struggle in the village nonetheless. People were responding in everyday ways to material deprivation and threats to their livelihood. What he witnessed amounted to examples of "the prosaic but constant struggle between the peasantry and those who seek to extract labor, food, taxes, rents, and interest from them."[10] In general, such struggle can include things like "foot dragging, dissimulation, desertion, false compliance, pilfering, feigned ignorance, slander, arson, sabotage, and so on."[11] And in contrast with the kinds of formally organized activities we usually think of as constituting social movements, the activities of everyday resistance generally "require little or no coordination or planning; they make use of implicit understandings and informal networks; they often represent a form of individual self-help; they typically avoid direct, symbolic confrontation with authority."[12] These activities included elaborate dynamics that were mostly polite and overtly obedient but involved a range of actions by the poorer members of the village to intervene in how wages were set and how non-wage distribution of resources took place. This was material, a struggle to get much needed food and wages and redistribution, and it was in part conducted by the aforementioned foot dragging, absence, and theft. But it was also cultural, as people in the village utilized conversation and gossip to mobilize shared values, norms, and stories as part of a struggle that was not only about resources but also about how practices related to resources, redistribution, and communal care should be understood and enacted.

All of these are, without a doubt, weapons of the weak. They were largely either completely hidden from public view or enacted only when plausibly deniable as at all oppositional or resistant. They won no flashy victories. But in contextualizing everyday resistance in terms of the broader dynamics of peasant struggle, Scott found that it definitely had an impact. The reluctance to take up more confrontational and visibly collective modes of struggle among most peasants in most times and places is, Scott argues, about a calculation based on the kind of repression they would face if they did. But in this distributed, uncoordinated, often invisible response by networks of individuals facing similar indignities and harms, and listening as best they could to their own circumstances, Scott argues that peasants have the effect of putting the brakes on the power of the landlords, tax collectors, and states that dominate their lives and creating a little more space, a little more possibility for living.

More everyday resistance

It is not always obvious whether a particular everyday action constitutes resistance in any meaningful sense. Nonetheless, there are some instances that are clear when we think about our own lives and about what we hear from other people. When I think back to the careful security measures in my long-ago gas station job that were aimed at stopping me from stealing a chocolate bar, those measures were probably in place because attendants in earlier years had responded to their poverty wages (and broader mistreatment) with a little bit of subsistence-by-theft. Whether you-the-reader likes or approves of this or not, it is everyday resistance as Scott understands it. It is common for acts of everyday resistance to be criminalized or condemned in dominant legal or moral frameworks that see the norms imposed by the oppressor as sacred and the lives of the oppressed as less valuable, even disposable. Hegemonic ideas can exert a powerful hold so it's not always the case, but at least sometimes, oppressed people have rather different frameworks for understanding what is necessary for survival, what is just, what is virtuous.

With a bit more breadth and depth of view and some historical perspective, it is possible to identify many other examples. Take the work of movement historian Robin D.G. Kelley. One chapter in his book *Race Rebels* talks about how a diverse range of cultural activities undertaken by working-class African Americans under the segregationist Jim Crow regime in the southern US in the first half of the twentieth century constituted a form of everyday resistance.[13] In both the daytime, sacred context of Black churches, and the nighttime, secular contexts of dance halls, gin joints, and other institutions of nightlife, "African American working people created a rich, dynamic culture that served as both a window into a hidden consciousness and a 'weapon of the weak.'"[14] Some of that was about seeking the solace, support, and righteous motivation of faith. Some of it was about making spaces to be able to mutually name their experiences in a world that, decades after slavery, still regarded Black bodies as objects from which to extract labour. Some of it was about engaging in a wide range of activities that refused that logic of objecthood and "enabled African Americans to take back their bodies for their own pleasure rather than another's profit."[15] It included choices about clothing and aesthetics made "as an assertion of dignity and resistance."[16] In all these ways, a sense of shared lives, of solidarity, was built. It was not, Kelley argues, just shared oppression that built the kind of solidarity that manifested more visibly when struggle took a collective form or in the kind of never-ending mutual aid within communities that ensured survival — it was a result of the many small, everyday moments of conversation, of building spaces to be together in leisure and pleasure and faith and community.

In another chapter, Kelley examines everyday resistance in the context of the public transit system in Birmingham, Alabama, in the 1940s.[17] In those years, the transit system was segregated — white people rode in the front of the bus, and African American people at the back. Buses were an ongoing site of friction and conflict, a site of all manner of everyday indignity imposed on African Americans. Bus drivers were armed, and often some of the white passengers were too, and there was plenty of both official and vigilante energy focused on keeping Black people in what was supposedly their place — and in turn, much need for African American passengers to make choices about how to act in the midst and aftermath of such indignities. Sometimes, those choices took a clearly resistant turn, including arguing, refusing to move when told, physical conflict, or refusal to pay all or part of the fare. Sometimes, it involved talking loudly to other Black passengers about the racist behaviour of whites. Sometimes, it involved humour at the expense of the oppressor. In some moments, this resistance was clearly a response to some immediate racist indignity. At other moments, it was more complicated, with, for example, young men being aggressive and defiant as a way to assert a masculinized personhood so often denied them and to take up public space. In contrast to the more deliberate civil rights campaigns that are more clearly remembered these many decades later, none of this was coordinated or planned or organized. While often these instances of everyday resistance did not end well, they did sometimes result in some immediate gain. As Kelley observed, "small victories were indeed possible."[18] More broadly, "unorganized, seemingly powerless black passengers made governing public transit more difficult by their acts of transgression,"[19] making it one context among many others in which everyday resistance made it harder to administer and enforce organized white supremacy.

One of the most compelling instances of everyday resistance described by Kelley in his book is not drawn from his historical research but from his own experience as an employee in a McDonald's restaurant in the late 1970s.[20] The supervisors were constantly pressuring them to do more, to work faster, to smile more. The customers were often unpleasant to the mostly Black and Latinx workers. "But," he wrote, "we found ways to compensate":

> Like virtually all of my fellow workers, I liberated McDonaldland cookies by the boxful, volunteered to clean "lots and lobbies" in order to talk to my friends, and accidentally cooked too many Quarter Pounders and apple pies near closing time, knowing fully well that we could take home whatever was left over.[21]

They set the shake machine to mess up to get some free milkshake, turned fifteen-minute breaks into twenty-five-minute breaks, fought to have *their* tunes on the radio rather than the easy listening dictated by management, insisted on wearing their hair in all the ways that Black people wear their hair despite whatever the employee handbook might say, and did what they could to make the labour process their own. None of this was done with any kind of deliberate, formal collectivity, though it was possible because of the informal relationships among the workers. Nor, according to Kelley, did they really think of themselves explicitly as workers fighting for their rights. It was, rather, young women and men doing things in an everyday way, in the midst and aftermath of injustice, to take back a little power, a little space, a little dignity in a dignity-denying workplace.

Another author who draws on the idea of everyday resistance is sociologist Patricia Hill Collins in *Black Feminist Thought,* her synthesis and summary of the feminisms enacted by Black women.[22] Though the phrase "everyday resistance" is used explicitly only a couple of times, the entire orientation of the book makes it clear that the everyday practices of Black women in the face of the ongoing harms and indignities of patriarchal white supremacy are both themselves often acts of resistance and the foundation upon which more visibly collective and confrontational resistance has been built in many different ways over many years. A pivotal element of how she understands resistance by Black women is that it has historically often required seeming to conform, due to the material risks in doing anything else, while simultaneously developing a resistant consciousness. Part of what Black women face is a range of vicious and awful stereotypes — what Hill Collins characterizes as "controlling images"[23] — and part of the everyday resistance of many Black women is developing a consciousness and self-definition that refuses those controlling images. This often extends to Black women playing an important role in teaching Black children in their communities, particularly Black girls, how to navigate and resist oppression.[24] More broadly, Hill Collins' expansive sense of the everyday practices that fall under the rubric of resistance extends, at least provisionally, to the wide range of "unacknowledged yet essential actions taken by countless US Black women to ensure [Black family and community] survival"[25] in the face of a system that wanted anything but — to the everyday labour, that is, of reproducing Black communities. The self-focused consciousness work is "essential"[26] to Black women's involvement in other kinds of efforts to make change, and without the broader set of practices of everyday resistance, more formal forms of "resistance to racial and class oppression could not have occurred."[27]

This resonates with the observation by historian Jennifer Lynn Stoever that in the context of slavery and harsh racial oppression in the nineteenth century, "black subjects began to decolonize their listening practices."[28] She argues that "crafting liberatory listening practices was … an important part of antiracist struggle."[29] In other words, in certain contexts, developing practices of listening that refuse the training into dominant affective, conceptual, and habitual modes of responsiveness that deny systemic oppression and reinforce the status quo, and that are premised on the listener's own dehumanization, can itself be a form of everyday resistance, and one not readily observable by anyone else.

Another rich set of examples can be found in Asef Bayat's book *Life as Politics: How Ordinary People Change the Middle East,* which examines resistance in the Muslim Middle East, particularly in Egypt and Iran.[30] Compared to the countries of the Global North, he argues, these and many other Global South countries feature political landscapes with substantively less space for formally organized, openly collective movements working in opposition to state policy. Such movements do sometimes happen in these countries, of course, but the constitutive level of repression they face is higher, so they are mostly less present. In their stead, he states, you often find widespread resistance in everyday contexts that is not formally coordinated but that nonetheless can be tremendously effective in cumulatively winning significant amounts of physical space, social space, and resources. He points to the urban poor in Cairo illegally taking land to build dwellings, taking over street corners to sell merchandise, taking over parts of streets to sell their services parking cars, and hooking up their homes and communities to electricity and other municipal services without permission. He talks as well about women at the individual level engaging in aspects of education, work, arts, music, sport, and other activities in and of everyday life in the face of barriers set by patriarchal elites and dominant norms. The "mundane doings" that constitute all this resistance "had perhaps little resemblance to extraordinary acts of defiance but rather were closely tied to the ordinary practices of everyday life."[31] And yet they were "essentially contentious and often extralegal practices that subvert governing norms and laws and infringe on power, property, and public"[32] and enhance the survival and thriving of oppressed groups.

in the context of relations

I said at the start of this chapter that while we listen and respond to experiences of indignity and harm in specific, concrete moments, we cannot understand those moments outside of the context of the listening-mediated social relations that produce them. We can think about this in lots of different ways. Sometimes, it is useful to do so narrowly — for instance, we can ask if what is happening in a given moment is actually harm in the sense we have been discussing it.

When viewed from outside of their relational context, accountability can look like harm, redistribution can look like harm, justice can look like harm. Take someone who is in an institutionally sanctioned relation of power over other people — an employer, a police officer, a faith leader — who uses the power of their position to inflict direct harm on somebody. Far too often, such people face no consequences. Sometimes, though, they do, perhaps through loss of position, income, or prestige. In a technical sense, they are being harmed — it can certainly feel like that to them, and that's how it looks if you just examine the moment and not the relational context in which the moment happens. But loss of a position or income because you are being held accountable for something terrible you have done is not at all the same as the moments of harm we are concerned about in this chapter and not at all the same as the harm that such people are being held accountable for. You can apply similar logic to many other situations as well. The shareholders who receive smaller dividends because a union won a strike and forced the corporation to put more money into safety precautions and into the pockets of workers have in a technical sense been harmed, because they have been deprived of resources that would otherwise be theirs. But in that circumstance — in the context of unjust relations — it is a good thing, a just thing, a thing that points towards a better world. There is a certain strand of thinking that argues for just outcomes by claiming that they are universally positive, that we will all be better off (and, implicitly, that no one will be harmed) if injustice X or Y is resolved. Sometimes that is true — having the legal right to visit your same-sex partner when they are in intensive care does not take anything away from anyone else, for example. But sometimes, just outcomes redistribute resources, restrict impunity, curb privilege, or completely up-end social relations that had previously awarded some people unearned advantage, and thereby technically cause harm to those people by taking from them that which they should not have had to begin with.

The same kind of immediate context matters for understanding people's actions. I already made the point that we should avoid decontextualized moralizing about how people navigate oppressive circumstances — it is at best unhelpful and often makes things worse. But all those details still matter to accurately understand and name what is happening. For example, if you have experienced harm, and part of how you deal with that is by harming someone else whom you have power over, that is "doing harm" in the sense that we are discussing it. Everyday navigation of oppressive circumstances can certainly involve taking space or resources in some way, but doing those kinds of things is only everyday *resistance* if it involves punching up, i.e., taking them from the landlord, or the employer, or the state, or whoever has power in the situation. If it involves taking from a neighbour or from someone even more marginalized, then whatever is going on, it is not resistance.

These conversations are not necessarily easy ones. It is certainly possible to come up with examples that are clear, but lots of the time when we encounter them in the course of life and struggle, they are anything but. If you are part of a community or movement where members have acted oppressively towards one another, figuring out what these things mean, not in some abstracted sense but in practice, is hard, hard work. I am no expert, but I would point people in the direction of the important thinking that abolitionist and transformative justice activists, prominently including those who understand themselves as feminists, have done around these things.[33]

It can also be important to think about moments of indignity and harm in a broader social relational context. In trying to articulate how that broader context matters, we could try to break it into discrete factors and variables, into reified models that simplify and extract. We could talk separately about risk, about opportunity, about the material resources a person can draw on, about the cultural resources at their disposal, about the repertoire of practices they have learned, about whatever innovation they can manage in the space they have. But that is not how we live it — we live it as a whole. Yet within that whole, those specifics — shaped by the particular social relations that have produced the person and produced the moment — mean that I face different moments of indignity and harm than you and I navigate them differently, with different outcomes. It means that the everyday resistance by fast food workers in a particular restaurant four decades ago, by the urban poor in Cairo, and by Black women in the US in the decades after slavery ended all looked different because they faced different kinds of indignity and harm, different risks, and different opportunities, and they had different practical and cultural resources to draw on.

Connection to different contexts and histories makes for different landscapes for taking action, provides different repertoires of resistance practices, and means that ostensibly similar acts can have different meanings and that people in otherwise similar situations might do different things. The swagger and space-taking of some young Black men on buses in Alabama in the 1940s, as documented by Kelley, was happening in the context of Jim Crow and legacies of slavery and all the social meaning — histories of oppression, resources for resistance — that were part of Black experience in that era. Young white men acting in superficially similar ways on a bus in my city today would and should be understood much differently. As Kelley makes clear, the resistance by fast food workers described above was also different from his experience in another McDonald's he worked in back then where the composition of the workforce was different — whiter, less poor — and it is likely that it would be different in a McDonald's today, after an additional forty years of concerted effort by the corporate behemoth to refine neoliberal techniques of management and control.

Careful attention to context can also help us appreciate the limits of everyday resistance as a framework for talking about the things people do in the face of indignity and harm. A different kind of example can be found through Nishnaabeg scholar and activist Leanne Betasamosake Simpson's book *As We Have Always Done*.[34] To understand Indigenous political resurgence, Simpson explores how Indigenous resistance is often grounded in place- and practice-based approaches to theorizing, to thinking, and to living. For her own people, she calls it "Nishnaabewin,"[35] and also draws on the language of "grounded normativity" from the work of Dene scholar Glen Coulthard.[36] The land in a given place, the practices of people living on that land, and the meaning and stories people generate in the course of living form a dense practical nexus of theorizing the world and how to live in it. It is a material grounding for logics of living other than those enforced by the dominant oppressive social relations in so-called Canada today. She argues that while centuries of settler colonial violence have done immeasurable harm to them, the grounded normativities of many Indigenous nations still survive and still provide a way to situate and guide nation-specific Indigenous ways of living and engaging in struggle. For Simpson, living according to Nishnaabewin "means struggle. Struggle because we are occupied, erased, displaced, and disconnected. Struggle because our bodies are still targets for settler colonial violence. Struggle because this is the mechanism our Ancestors engaged in to continuously rebirth the world."[37] In particular, it is struggle that does not necessarily prioritize confrontation (though that does happen sometimes) but rather often works through withdrawal from dominant social logics into logics of Nishnaabewin, which she names "Biiskabiyang — the process of returning to ourselves, a reengagement with the things we have left behind, a reemergence, an unfolding from the inside out."[38] All of this means that, in the context of moments of indignity and harm, at least some Indigenous people are drawing on distinct cultural resources and visions for possible future worlds, which will both shape their actions in those moments and contribute to those actions both doing and meaning different things than everyday resistance by people situated in other ways. At least in some contexts, it is arguable that the language of "everyday resistance" itself is not a good fit, and something more suited to the relevant grounded normativity would be a better way to talk about such practices.

what everyday resistance is and what it isn't

We have to be realistic about what everyday resistance can and cannot do. Today, there are still plenty of people, including people involved in or writing about social movements, who have no interest in paying attention to how people listen and act in their everyday lives in the face of oppression, including how they resist. Yet as we have seen from the examples in this chapter, everyday resistance can lead to both small but meaningful gains in the moment and to cumulative impacts. On the individual level, liberating some grain from your landlord so your family has enough to eat, seizing a little corner of public space on a Cairo street to sell your wares, or making sure your daughter is as equipped as possible to navigate the anti-Black racism and sexism she will face as she grows up all contribute to at least surviving, perhaps thriving, and maybe even to future possibilities for other kinds of resistance. On a larger scale, the examples in this chapter show lots of ways in which the cumulative impact of everyday resistance makes a difference in the world, in some contexts restrains what oppressors can do to inflict indignity and harm, and ensures a little more space for living.

At the same time, there are also people who romanticize everyday resistance and exaggerate what it can do or expand its scope beyond what the evidence will bear. In the afterword in *Race Rebels,* Kelley notes that right from its release in the mid 1990s, lots of people misread the book: "Some of my critics and even my defenders mistakenly treated these stories of working-class struggle as superior modes of resistance for all times and places."[39] As well, in recent decades, particularly in academic contexts, some people have applied "everyday resistance" to actions that do not seem to meet the criteria I am using here — they have included acts that have a flavour or an echo or a resonance of resistance in them but do not have the kinds of relationships to direct benefit, to material impact, or to other forms of resistance outlined in the examples in this chapter. This connects to Bayat's insistence in *Life as Politics* on defining what he is talking about as "nonmovements" and as meaningfully distinct from "everyday resistance." I suspect this is to make clear that he is describing a phenomenon that is not captured by the less grounded way in which the latter term sometimes gets used.[40] Personally, I can only offer anecdotal evidence, but it feels like I have run across something similar. I'm thinking of things like young middle-class anarchists who romanticize working-class people engaging in everyday sabotage or theft without appreciating their risks or limits, or graduate students who develop arguments that exaggerate the extent to which an obscure cultural intervention is meaningful resistance. I suspect the tendency to overestimate what everyday resistance can accomplish and to take acts that seem to be resistant and give them political meaning detached from their context has something to do with decades of enculturation to the individualized thinking pushed by neoliberalism and also to do with decades of our movements frequently losing and the understandable need to find inspiration where we can.

Whatever the source of such misunderstandings, we need to re-focus on the reality that everyday resistance, even when understood in careful and grounded ways, remains a way of naming actions that, while they indeed do have an impact on lives and on worlds, by their very nature have serious limits. Harms might be mitigated, some space and resources might be won, oppressed communities might be more able to survive in an environment organized to destroy them, dominant norms might be gradually shifted, the ground might be prepared for other kinds of struggle, and all these things matter tremendously. But on its own, everyday resistance will not re-make the social relations that created the harm and indignity in the first place, and we are not doing ourselves or anyone else any favours if we refuse to recognize its limits. Again, quoting Kelley, everyday resistance is "not ... some alternative to organized social movements."[41] Sometimes, as people listen to the moments of indignity and harm that fill their lives, they resist in the everyday and still yearn for more. That is where we turn our attention now.

chapter seven

collective movements

Imagine people who are navigating harm in their everyday lives. They don't do it alone, necessarily — they are in relation, after all, so they talk, they share some things, they support each other. Situated as they are, they often manage to get on with life and assert their dignity and claim joy in a world that denies these things. They comply when they must, and they resist when they can. Maybe that continues indefinitely, because they can see no prospect for anything else. Maybe they're right about that. But maybe, just maybe, they reach a point where resistance beyond this feels imaginable, necessary. In response to some circumstance changed or threshold passed, one or a few or all of them want resistance that goes beyond what they can do within the constraints of their currently existing everyday lives. So, what do they do? And what role does listening play?

beyond everyday resistance

We know what it looks like to resist beyond the everyday.[1] Or we think we know, anyway. Perhaps we gather in a group, carry signs, listen to speeches, chant and sing. Perhaps we take to the streets, and we march. At city hall, in a public square, at the corporate headquarters or the federal building, we collectively channel anger or grief. We demand an end to harm and the beginnings of a better world. Or maybe, together, we withhold our labour, we picket, we strike. We tell our bosses that we will not accept their mistreatment, their disregard for our safety, their theft of what should be ours, and they will not profit from our work until they make things right. To the extent that we see struggles for justice represented in the media, it often looks like one of these things. But resistance can take a lot of other forms, too.

Resistance often looks like sitting around a table — endlessly[2] talking, debating, arguing, tears, yelling, calm words, good points, reassurance, sharing, support, affirmation, care, ideas bouncing, energizing rants, hard-won agreement, consensus. Within our movements and communities, *this* is perhaps the biggest part of the work. It is sitting in a room with people you like, people you don't like, people you agree with, people who are so incredibly wrong you can hardly stand it, and figuring out what to do next. Sometimes it is agonizing, disjointed, ineffective, filled with mansplaining and off-topic rambling. But, equally, there can be a synergy, a coming together, a creation of something new that is not me, not you, not them, but *us*. The group is focused, the goal is clear, we make it work, and the struggle advances an inch or two.

Or maybe it is a small group gathered at the constituency office, the ministry, the place of assembly, or some other building where the relations that comprise the state form tell us power resides. They deploy demands, facts, arguments to sway some politician or bureaucrat, with the implicit threat that the next election might well depend on whether they listen.

Perhaps it is a mode of resistance that involves knowing, telling, making, sharing. It is people who face overlapping traumas sitting together, talking through their experiences, realizing they are not alone, that it is not a private failing but a political problem that can be solved by acting together.[3] It is building community knowledge about an issue through teach-ins, media work, posters, flyers. It is creating a space for those in the movement to discuss and debate, to reflect on success and failure, to share histories and theory.[4] It is doing research, building knowledge, writing reports in movement-grounded ways that serve as tools to advance the cause.[5] Or it is sharing the practical skills that make resistance possible.[6]

It may be bodies taking space, disrupting, preventing, reclaiming, protecting. You take over the meeting, stop it from proceeding. Your MLA's staff politely dismiss you, and you refuse to leave the office until the police drag you out.[7] Or it is your land, it has always been your land, no matter how many times the colonial courts ratify the colonial theft, so you stand on it, you build on it, you live on it, you refuse to leave.[8] You physically block the pipeline crews, or the bulldozers, or the gates of the company making weapons, or the route necessary for the deportation.[9] Or you march but you don't just march — you block, you disrupt, business will not proceed as usual while they continue to kill Black people with impunity. They are evicting homeless people from encampments, claiming this will move people into real housing, claiming the shelter system is adequate and safe, and it is lies and lies and lies, so you gather and try, in the face of batons and pepper spray and the system's willingness to shed blood, to stop them.[10]

It is a language nest. You, and a cousin, and a close friend, and a handful strangers — a teacher and some learners — living together for a month, speaking (as best you can) only the language that Canada has unsuccessfully tried to steal, tried to kill. You connect with each other, connect with the land, connect with the words, connect with the ways of being embedded in all of that. Or, perhaps, it is less focused, more distributed.[11] Perhaps it is old-new activities, practices, events, ceremonies — old, but new to you, new to others — in your community. Perhaps it is learning that doesn't feel like learning, sitting around a kitchen table, in a community hall, in the woods, on a bus.[12] Whatever form it takes, it is invisible from outside, but you can feel it — strengthened roots that mean the tree of your people will flourish, stand more defiantly, be more able to refuse the colonizer in ways big and little.

There are a lot of things like that — activities that do not look like what many of us assume resistance looks like but that nonetheless are resistance. Often, I think, it is communities-in-struggle acting together in resistant ways that grow from everyday resistance and that those of us raised in privilege misrecognize, define out of relevance, ignore. I know there is a whole broad field that I might not notice, might not understand as resistance, even if it was right in front of me.

Sometimes, resistance looks like picking up the gun, insurrection, revolution in one of its more traditional guises or perhaps in some totally new form. What that might mean and what it might look like, when the world we so fervently desire is one in which all live with dignity and free from harm, is a hard, complicated thing. There are some who embrace a vision of change in which the implications of such modes of struggle are romanticized and caricatured. But we live in a harsh and violent world, a world of systems and relations that are so stubbornly stable and so able to adapt their terrible grip, a world in which states and their agents resort to violence so readily to preserve injustice, a world that so constrains what people can do and imagine and how they can live, that such modes of struggle can become thinkable, can feel inevitable, can sometimes seem to be the only path forward.

collectivity and reconfigured relationships

Clearly, then, resistance that goes beyond everyday resistance can look like a lot of different things, some of which I name above, but many more of which I have no doubt missed entirely. Even those that I do mention encompass a lot of different things. For those of us who have spent years going to them, a rally or march may seem to be the most stereotypical, unoriginal, and ordinary way imaginable of manifesting a collective desire for change. But in terms of how it is organized, the demands it advances, the role it plays in broader strategy, its relationship to longer-standing formations, the risk involved, the specific tactics employed along the way, its political implications, the likely response by state authorities, and much more, a march can be — perhaps isn't often, but can be — many different things.

Given the breadth of what resistance can look like, it is probably no shock at all that there is not just one path through which it all happens. The ways you go about bringing together a handful of Indigenous language learners and teachers on the land looks different than circumstances producing a spontaneous upsurge of collective rage taking over a city square, which looks different than putting together a series of meetings to plan a new feminist initiative against sexual assault. It is perhaps a bit risky, then, to make any generalizations at all about how resistance happens, especially given my acknowledgement that my own imagining of such things is probably far from complete. But I think there are a couple that are safe enough.

The first of these generalizations is that, whatever form it takes, however it happens, resistance that goes beyond the everyday is *collective*. That's not to imply by contrast that everyday resistance is solitary, of course. We already talked about how it happens in relational contexts, and even when it is one person's act, it cannot be understood by thinking about that person or that moment in isolation. But, even so, there is also something about more-than-everyday resistance that is clearly connected to people doing things together in a way that is both novel and deliberate.

This matters. The individualism that dominates our culture may hide this from us, may denigrate it, but collectivity is powerful.[13] I think of moments I have had over the years when I have been busily working away on some task as part of a small grassroots group and I have been profoundly struck by how much we are able to accomplish. Even just half a dozen people working together smoothly and well, who know each other and have a range of complementary skills, can do far more than half a dozen individuals working on their own or passively coordinated towards parallel actions via an online platform. Of course, a glance at history shows that, together, large numbers can accomplish orders of magnitude more, can win victories that no one thought possible, can transform what was previously seen as unchanging and eternal — can end slavery, can win the vote, can overturn governments, and on, and on. Sure, groups are often also dysfunctional and internally oppressive and unstrategic and as foolish as the humans that comprise them. As well, the power of collectivity can just as easily be directed at destructive ends as liberatory ones. But, undeniably, acting with others has the potential to not just add our efforts together but to amplify and multiply them. As Vancouver-based migrant justice organizer Harsha Walia has put it, "There is no liberation in isolation; indeed, there is no liberation *possible* in isolation."[14]

The other generalization I feel comfortable making is that, whatever its specifics look like, resistance beyond what is possible in your existing everyday life happens because relationships get reconfigured in some way. That is maybe not a very intuitive way of characterizing what happens, so let me talk it through in a bit more detail. It is worth going back over some ground we covered earlier. We talked plenty about how we all exist in relation with one another, whether we want to or not. I may never meet you, but we are both woven into the broad socially organized relations that, in the twenty-first century, wrap the globe. There are also ways we are in somewhat more specific, though still indirect, relation. You are, after all, reading this book. Right now, as I type, I am writing it. At other times and in other places, people edited it, people printed it, people wrote promotional copy, people talked it up to their friends (I hope — hint hint!). All those people are placed in a particular kind of relation through this book. The same is true of all the other ways the activities of other people feed into, make possible, and inform our lives, and our activities do the same for others. We can move still closer to our immediate experience — we are in various kinds of relation with our family, our friends, our co-workers, the people who work in stores we go to, and so on. In a fundamental sense, these relations produce our everyday experiences, including experiences of indignity and harm, and are the context in which we enact our everyday complicity, everyday solidarity, everyday resistance, and all the rest.

Any instance of resistance I can think of that goes beyond everyday resistance involves some kind of shift, some kind of re-configuration, of some of these relationships. Say you and a couple of co-workers are talking during your break and you realize that a decision your manager made isn't fair. You talk to a few other co-workers, and, as a group, you go to her office and say your piece. You were already in relation through the social organization of the workplace, but in subtle but important ways you have taken action to shift those relations in a way that makes you more able to collectively intervene with respect to something that matters in your lives. Where it goes from there, of course, is anybody's guess. Maybe your manager is shocked and changes her decision or maybe she laughs and threatens you with disciplinary action, and that new collectivity dissipates and the workplace is back to what it was before. Or, perhaps, there is a tense standoff, and this is only the beginning of something much larger, of ongoing conflict and of an enduring and militant collectivity.

Or say the resistance is ten thousand people gathered in a city square in rage and solidarity for an afternoon. It may be transient, but it too is an example of relations reconfiguring in a way that makes a new kind of resistance possible. Or imagine a high-rise apartment building — in a way analogous to the workplace example, its residents start out in relation through shared space and similar experiences of exploitation and mistreatment by the real estate investment trust that owns the building, but they can become a committee or a tenant union able to exert collective power in the face of it all.

I raise one more example because I think its distinctiveness is important to understand.[15] Take a highly oppressed community that has a dense web of relationships already — maybe an Indigenous reserve, maybe an African Nova Scotian community, maybe something else. The people in this community already do plenty of everyday resistance, in ways dependent on that existing web of relations. But say a few kids in the community get treated in racist ways by school officials. The dense web of relationships already exists, certain practices of supporting each other already exist, and the community has acted in more overtly collective ways to stand up for themselves plenty of times in the last couple of hundred years. But, still, when folks get together in the church basement to talk about what to do in response to those racist school officials, that too is a reconfiguration of relationships. It is a fluid one, a familiar one, one that is a product of hard-won past experience, and it doesn't require starting from scratch like for many workers or tenants. But it is still a subtle shift in how people are in relation with one another with an eye towards more deliberately exerting collective power.

Another way to talk about reconfiguring relationships is as bringing people together to form a new *we* or as changing things, subtly or dramatically, in an existing *we*. This new or changed *we* might, as I said, be fleeting and exist in its new relational form for only an afternoon, or it might be an organization that ends up lasting a century. It might involve a million people, or it might involve three people. It might be a formal entity with rules and bylaws and name tags, or it might be an informal cluster of people with nebulous practices and boundaries. It might involve deep enmeshment of lives, or it might be shallow togetherness in space or practice. But it is people, newly or differently together, acting to make change.

the work of resistance

Even in this individualistic, atomized, neoliberal age, people exist as part of instances of *we* across the gamut of form, formality, purpose, and size, and in every sphere of life. Think families and basketball teams, widget corporations and choirs, fandoms and street gangs, multi-level marketing schemes and government departments. Instances of *we* that are specifically oriented to exerting collective power are not necessarily any different than any of the rest in how they form, change, grow, or dissipate. Given that, it is tempting to refuse to define it further, to stand and point at everything human beings do and just shrug. A new *we* or a change in an existing *we* happens in all the ways people relate to people, relationships form and deepen and grow, activities are socially coordinated and organized, bodies are brought together in space or in feeling, trust emerges and collaboration intensifies, ideas and practices spread, and people work together. To understand how a new *we* or a changed *we* oriented towards resistance comes about and takes action, we do not need to treat it as something strange or separate. Rather, we need to listen to the social ebb and flow that surrounds us and apply what we learn to the problem at hand.

As honest and true as that way of thinking about it may be, however, it is not necessarily helpful on its own.

Some of how relationships reconfigure, in life as a whole and in this specific domain, is in response to changes in circumstance or context that are beyond our control, beyond our capacity to anticipate. There is a push or a pull, something new being done or some new possibility for doing, some change yesterday for one reason that means we can or must act differently along another axis today. This never fully explains when and how new forms of resistance emerge, but it is part of the mix.

This is true at the small and local scale — the cops brutalize a local community member and his neighbours protest, or your landlord hikes the rent one too many times and you and your fellow tenants organize a rent strike. It is also true of the great, sudden upsurges we have semi-regularly seen in the last fifteen years — from Idle No More, through Occupy and the multiple uprisings against anti-Black police violence, as well as the wave of actions to #ShutDownCanada in solidarity with Wet'suwet'en land defenders, and the global wave of opposition to the Israeli state's genocidal assault on Gaza. In each of those, there was some threat, some new tactic, some horrific act, some expanded sense of possibility, some combination thereof, and people came together in their thousands, their millions, and created a new *we*, at least for a little while (and often many smaller collectivities that long outlasted the phase of the upsurge visible through the mainstream media). Relationships reconfigure and the new or changed *we* acts.

That's not the whole story, though. However they might be catalyzed, facilitated, or socially organized and whatever action they might take, the ways people are in relation with each other and the ways they act together are also a product of work on the part of the people involved. Note that I mean "work" in its broadest sense, as all the many things we do every day to collectively make the world. Whether you are talking about a recreational sports team, a community of worship, or the take-no-prisoners trio of you and your besties, the things we do (within the constraints we face) make those relationships happen, make them form, make them change, make them end, and are how we collectively impact the world. The form and direction of that work is inevitably organized by more than whatever might lie in individual hearts, but that work is what makes it happen.

When I think about the work that might be involved in bringing people together in ways oriented to building collective power and making change, the word that springs to mind is "organizing." Admittedly, it is a bit of a slippery word, as even people actively engaged in movements and communities-in-struggle use it in wildly different ways. Some people talk about any change-oriented collective activity as "organizing" regardless of what it involves. As well, even those activities that are more obviously organizing in its precise sense — i.e., bringing people together in some social form meant to effectively engage in struggle — still cover a broad range and can be open to plenty of critique, whether because of the methods used, the kinds of social forms created, or more generally. All of that aside, though, organizing is one important way of naming the kind of work I'm talking about.

Still, I am not sure the label "organizing" effectively captures *all* such work. As important as I think organizing is, I want to at least partially set it aside as a way of framing what I am saying here — I worry that it might get in the way of noticing what is actually going on when we come together (or come together differently) to make change and that it might end up functioning as a gatekeeping mechanism where we define particular instances of *we* as not legitimate or not worth talking about because they do not look like what we are expecting.[16] Whether the sequence of events fits our definition of organizing or not, what kind of work is happening as relationships reconfigure and people act together to fight for change?

Even just starting from more to-me conventional ways this might happen, it is possible to identify many kinds of work. Feeling hurt or outrage or anger or grief.[17] Talking to others about experiences and feelings, ours and theirs. Making a decision to do something more than we've done before. Reaching out to others to see if they are interested, figuring out common ground, hearing their concerns, their thoughts, their doubts. Meeting. Planning. Debating big-picture strategy, deciding on goals and tactics. Writing a callout for action and circulating it far and wide. Working out logistics, figuring out how to implement them, and implementing them. Using our knowledge and skills to build a latrine, safely block a railway line, cook, draw, design, compose. Facilitating a meeting or doing the kind of informal but crucial people-work that is essential to relationships of whatever sort. Organizing and delivering care for the children of other participants. Making a leaflet, handing it out on a street corner, and navigating the resulting conversations to maximize the likelihood of passersby attending the upcoming action. You might spend a lot of time sitting with movement or community elders and taking up how they challenge you as you figure out a plan of action. You make a sign, convince your mom that you'll be safe, yell your heart out once you're there, and post a photo to social media in hopes your younger cousins see and take an interest — you aren't an organizer, but all those activities are work that went into making the march a success. You mask up with a few close comrades and disable some earth-destroying equipment, which is premised on all kinds of prior relational work to build trust as well as security practices and technical know-how. You do the research. You make the slides. You give the talk. You plan, promote, and deliver the pre-action training. You talk your fellow organizer through their freak-out. You lock down all your social media and move for a couple of weeks, because some right-wing grifter pretending to be a journalist has pointed the outrage-and-abuse machine in your direction. You wash the dishes, pick up the trash, turn off the lights, write some thank-you notes, send out the reminder for the follow-up meeting. You have a celebratory potluck — more planning, more cooking, more care — because, dammit, you won. All those different kinds of doing (and many others besides) are the work that make and change *we* and that act to create change in the broader world.

the work of listening

Woven through all this other work is the work of listening, just as it is woven through every other aspect of the social world, every other domain of life. Sometimes, listening is present as a discrete task, identified and named. Most of the time, however, listening is not the *what* that must be debated and decided upon but is rather an integral part of the *how* of whatever is happening.

At the most basic level, any process of coming together and then acting collectively to make change involves listening. We listen to the world via our experiences of it, and we listen to other people — their actions and the knowledge, stories, feelings, and imagination they share through their communications. This is how we know about the injustices we face ourselves and about injustices that lie beyond our own experience, it is how we arrive at the realization that there is a need to make things different, and it is how we figure out what that might look like. It is how we build shared understandings and a commitment to shared doing with other people. It is how we form relationships, debate ideas, negotiate actions, and act. As we learn to do things we need to do for that work, as we intervene in the world, as we gauge what is going on around us in order to be more effective, as we ensure that our actions fit with those of our comrades, we listen. We listen as we do all the people-work, all the communications work, all the making work, all the deciding work, all the coordinating work that makes movements happen, that shapes the inevitably complicated dynamics of cohesion and power and struggle that happen within movements, that sometimes fracture and end movements. We listen to the impacts of our actions to better decide what we must do next.

The work of listening is also how movements have much of their impact on the world. Some of this is because movements develop a vision of change, a collection of stories, a set of values, a series of goals and demands, and then they communicate them directly or they take some symbolic actions that express them. Some people take those things in, take them up, and change their own thinking and doing accordingly. But much of the impact movements and communities-in-struggle have, and perhaps even most, is not through purely communicative, symbolic, or educational activities but through other kinds of interventions in the world. Often, it is through gathering a hundred thousand people together, or reclaiming a part of your nation's territory, or shutting down a factory, or blocking some critical infrastructure that the most impact is made. It is not just expressing opposition but defying and refusing and disrupting. It is not just publicly desiring otherwise; it is making sure, materially, that things will not continue as they are and opening practical space for the transformative and the new. Some of this impact is direct — it is the practical, physical consequence of bodies doing, or not doing, or enabling, or preventing. Even in the case of those kinds of actions, though, listening plays a big role in how they make change in the world. Through direct observation and via social, grassroots, and mainstream media, people take in, take up, and make meaning from such actions, and that too can be a crucial route of impact.[18] The way the strike prevents the company from making money matters to whether the workers will win, but so do the ways in which the rest of the community is listening to, talking about, and responding to it.

listening between movements

Along with the listening that weaves through how movements form and act in the world, aspects of how movements as collective social forms exist and act in relation with one another can be usefully understood through listening. Struggle circulates,[19] and it does so because those to whom it is circulating listen and respond. You can see that in the great upsurges I mentioned earlier. It is listening not just to some change in external circumstance that requires a response, but to the messages "We can!" and "We must!" from other places, and knowing it is true where you are too. Perhaps less obvious to people who are not actively engaged with movements, though, it is also listening to what has been effective there and that promises to be effective for you, from ways of occupying public space, to specific tactics, to particular political sensibilities.[20] In such moments, there can be an element of masses of people in motion creating the conditions of possibility for their own activities — a feedback loop in which more and more people listen and act, making the previously unthinkable into today's minimum demand. You can see this in a focused way in the uprising in the wake of the police murder of George Floyd in Minneapolis in 2020, where the slogan and sentiment of "defund the police" went from a fairly fringe politics in North America to one with considerable mainstream reach.[21] You can also see it in the great revolutionary moments of the past — 1789, 1848, 1968, and so on — in a generalized way.

Such moments can also include circulation of struggle from one movement into others. A classic example of this is the wave of struggle that swept the world in and around 1968.[22] It was an era defined by high levels of resistance of a lot of different sorts in a lot of different places. The anti-colonial struggle against the US presence in Vietnam had already taken on a powerful practical and symbolic role for many around the world, and the demonstration in that year's Tet offensive that poorly armed peasants could turn the tide against an imperial military with far superior technology supported by seemingly infinite wealth opened up whole new vistas of possibility and, according to historian George Katsiaficas, "inspired the global movement."[23] Often carried into new contexts by student mobilizations, this momentum combined with local histories of struggle like the Black freedom movement in the US and workers' struggles in many other places to spawn a rich diversity of new, larger, and transformed instances of *we*, leaving hardly a country untouched. The foment of 1968 also contributed to the emergence of new movements that would develop further in the coming years, like the new wave of women's liberation struggle in North America and elsewhere.

Another important context in which to see related dynamics is the long Black freedom struggle in the United States.[24] Some argue that Black organizing is not only crucial in its own right but, because of the specific features of social formation in the US, has often been a catalyst or driver for other forms of social struggle and that momentum and practices from the Black freedom movement have fed into and shaped many other movements. It was in part the growing momentum of the Black civil rights and then Black Power movements that created the space — imaginative, social, political — for the flowering of the many other kinds of liberation movements that emerged in the late 1960s.[25]

You can imagine the numerous ways such circulation happens in practice. People, in various senses, move. That might mean they stay rooted in different contexts, but they encounter one another and communicate — speak, listen — in all the ways people do. Or it can mean that people who were involved in one place relocate to another and bring with them their histories and experiences, or that people who were involved in a different way in a prior moment bring that into the new thing happening here and now. Even when people stay in one place, images, stories, knowledge, and feelings circulate among us in a whole bunch of mediated ways. In all these scenarios, listening is central to the *how* of it.

Along with circulation of struggle as a general phenomenon, there can be particular kinds of ongoing, listening-mediated relationships between differently situated movements or communities-in-struggle. An important one involves relations of solidarity.[26] I am thinking, here, about relations of solidarity at the collective level, where some *we* decides, in all the complex, messy, not-all-deliberate ways that collectivities arrive at an orientation and set of practices, to act in solidarity. In his book *Solidarity: Hidden Histories and Geographies of Internationalism,* David Featherstone shows, particularly when it is not just the pronouncements of leaders but emerges from the actions and orientations of ordinary participants, that solidarity not only has the potential to change the circumstances of those on the receiving end but also creates the possibility that the movement enacting solidarity will itself emerge from that process changed in meaningful ways.[27] The book opens with an example that is profound but little remembered today.[28] During the US Civil War, the exigencies of war and a blockade by the Union led to a drastic drop in the amount of cotton grown in the Confederacy that made it to mills in England. There was significant sentiment among the English ruling class to intervene on the side of the Confederacy. But, though they were suffering themselves from the mass layoffs due to the lack of raw materials, some workers in the cotton mills and beyond mobilized in solidarity with the struggle to end slavery. Not only was this evidence of militant working-class support for the Union an element in the ultimate decision by the British Empire not to intervene directly in the war, but "these solidarities contributed to the founding of the International Working Men's Association (IMWA) in 1864,"[29] also called the First International, an important landmark in working-class movements in Europe and beyond. Featherstone shares many other examples of grassroots practices of solidarity that ended up shaping the world and also the further struggles of those who enacted them.

Movements are also shaped by collective listening through time. One element of this is indirect but profound, in the sense that movements are listening and responding to current circumstance and how things are in this moment is a product of struggles in the past. For example, the existence of public health care, education, and social programs in Canada — however partial those might be, however flawed, however bound up with colonialism, racism, and other oppressions — is an outcome of struggle by ordinary people in past generations. So, the many struggles today that are against austerity and government cuts to or privatization of these programs[30] and that are fighting to address the deep problems and gaps in the system[31] are shaped by listening, if not exactly to movements past, at least to the consequences of the struggles of those movements.

Then there are countless ways that listening to past movements more directly shapes those in the present. Certainly, people involved in struggle today could do more to listen to the lessons of the past — to challenge the "social organization of forgetting" with the "resistance of remembering," as radical scholar and anti-capitalist and queer liberation activist Gary Kinsman puts it[32] — but they often nonetheless do some. Through encounters, through the movement of people, and through the movement of knowledge and stories, ways of doing things and ways of thinking about the world filter down through time, and whether they are conscious of this listening to the past or not, those engaged in struggle today do listen. Sometimes, a group or movement or community-in-struggle might consciously situate itself in relation to a specific past movement and deliberately draw from it. People in an African Nova Scotian community might be drawing on their own community's traditions of struggle reaching back centuries, or members of a socialist group might be deliberate in choosing which elements of socialist tradition and practices they listen to as they make their decisions about action. It also happens in more ad hoc and contingent ways, with groups drawing on a whole range of traditions, some of which they are aware of and many others of which they are not, because to them these ideas and practices are simply part of the environment in which they are working. Grassroots anti-authoritarian politics in twenty-first-century North America have a fascinating braid of lineages, and you can trace strands of politics — "anti-racist feminism," "prison abolitionism," and "reconfigured anarchism" in one telling of it[33] — and strands of practices — affinity groups, consensus decision making, and much more — through movements extending back at least to the Second World War,[34] though many people active in these politics know little about that history.

listening and the harms of movements

We talked earlier about how power, oppression, and resistance can often be framed in terms of listening. This is true not only when we talk about what movements are fighting against in the broader world and the changes they strive to make but also about the ways in which movements themselves sometimes reproduce oppressive power. Social movements and communities-in-struggle may do important work towards liberation along one axis but still inflict indignity and harm, both internally and externally, along others. They are no worse in this regard than other social forms, and sometimes they are considerably better, but in general their starting point is the same social relations as the rest of the world.

Oppressive practices in movements can manifest in all manner of everyday indignities and harms imposed on prospective and existing participants — men talking over women in meetings, inaction on sexual harassment, ableist ways of working, movement demands based on assumptions about what the "real problem" is that clearly have not engaged with the experiences and analyses of anyone who is not white, unspoken norms of behaviour that mean that if you are queer or Muslim or working class you can never feel fully comfortable being yourself, and so much more. In a larger sense, the ways in which a movement as a collective enterprise listens and responds (or not) to the needs and voices of differently situated people, both within and beyond its own bounds, say a great deal about what that movement is actually doing in the world, how power is working within it, and what kind of change it might actually create as it wins victories.

Kevin Van Meter opens his book about everyday resistance with an anecdote that illustrates the unfortunate fact that it is all too easy for organizers to fail to be responsive to the needs and experiences of the people they are working with. He talks about doing door knocking in a predominantly racialized working-class community for a major anti-poverty organization, trying to sign people up and get donations for a campaign around childcare.[35] In terms of stats about poverty and availability of subsidized childcare spaces, this should have been a winning issue among the people in this neighbourhood. But most people they spoke to were not interested. They had, by and large, figured out ways to manage when it came to childcare, and it was just not a central focus of the struggles they were facing in their lives. However that organization developed its agenda, it was not by listening to the everyday experiences of the people it was trying to organize.

Similarly, sometimes labour bureaucrats have a different sense of what is necessary in a given situation than rank-and-file members, and they don't listen to the latter, which may well be in the context of organizational forms that enable that not-listening. Sometimes, those scrambling to cobble together funding in the not-for-profit sector — also sometimes called the non-profit industrial complex[36] — do so while facing different compulsions and constraints than those whose needs they are supposedly meeting, and they fail to listen to those everyday struggles. Political parties claiming to represent the marginalized and the downtrodden all too easily put their own electoral fortunes ahead of what their ostensible constituency actually needs and then claim pragmatism in a way that sounds virtuous when it is just another excuse for not listening. To the extent that parties do listen to those needs, it is frequently not to meet them but to manipulate and control, while listening much more devotedly to the booming voices of the rich and powerful. It can also be a question of who and what a given movement, organization, or group centres — perhaps it is grounded in responsiveness to the everyday experiences of people within its ambit but not to the most marginalized among them. Perhaps it is white, middle-class, cis queers whose everyday lives are listened to and centred in the 2SLGBTQI+ organization's work, rather than those of Black and Indigenous trans women and sex workers.

None of this is simple or inevitable, and it is not just a matter of dismissing the work and struggles of entire sectors or movements, just of recognizing that they are part of — within and against — the world they fight to change rather than acting from outside it. Collective strivings for justice and liberation can no more be pure than can the conduct of individuals.[37] Nonetheless, disconnection by some movement formations from everyday experience and resistance, particularly those of the most heavily oppressed, is a real phenomenon and a substantial barrier to true collective liberation.

Framing this in terms of listening is perhaps more clearly useful in this instance than it is when thinking about power in general, because it points towards what those of us in movements need to look for and what we can actually do. We can be constantly looking at the movements we are a part of and asking questions. It brings to mind the end of the book *BlackLife: Post-BLM and the Struggle for Freedom* by radical scholars Rinaldo Walcott and Idil Abdillahi.[38] In recognition that "Black people are dying in our cities, crossing oceans, in resource wars not of our making; in every conceivable area of life we are dying and dying in numbers disproportionate to others," it suggests something that the authors describe as the "Black Test."[39] In the context of "liberals' and the left's banal commitments to white supremacy,"[40] they write that the "Black Test simply suggests that any policy that does not meet the requirements of ameliorating the dire conditions of Black people's lives is not a policy worth having."[41] It sounds like an obvious point, but lots of what many groups, organizations, and movements do would not pass this test — so many are not grounded in, responsive to, listening to the voices and everyday struggles of, and collective struggles led by, Black people. It is important to maintain and honour the specificity of the Black Test. As so many Black activists, organizers, and radical thinkers have pointed out, it is easy for even anti-racist movements to fall into re-inscribing anti-Black racism through not bothering to name it or through adopting terminology that inappropriately generalizes. As well, many other movements in North America have learned or taken from Black movements and then failed to support them. But I think it is possible to maintain that specific attention while also learning from it more broadly and asking other questions as well. How do the goals, strategy, tactics, stories, knowledge, and forms of organization of a given movement relate to the everyday struggles of those within its public who face the greatest levels of indignity and harm? Is the movement in question led by Black people? Is it substantively guided by the needs, voices, and analyses of Black people? Indigenous Peoples? Trans people? Disabled people? Sex workers? People at the intersections of these identities? The point is not to ask that in an abstract way, in a way that might be answered by pointing to all the oppressed groups for whom we declare our solidarity in our mission statement but in a practical way. How does it show up in what our movements do and how we do it? What would it look like to reconfigure our relationships and our stories, to come together into a *we* that could more effectively exert collective power, with those facing the greatest levels of indignity and harm at the centre? What are our movements doing, in the words of Nishnaabeg writer and scholar Leanne Betasamosake Simpson, "to create the conditions where the lives of Indigenous and Black women and Two-Spirit, trans, and queer people are precious; where all living things are precious"?[42]

Beyond just asking questions, we can challenge the movements we are a part of (and those we are not a part of but that are active nearby) to do better. Such relations of challenge are another crucial form of listening-mediated relation within and between movements. A commonly cited example of such challenge is the emergence of the women's liberation movement in North America in the late 1960s and early 1970s. Women who were committed activists, organizers, and revolutionaries in various movements were facing all manner of sexist treatment and worse at the hands of men who were ostensibly their comrades.[43] Attempts to raise that within those spaces largely received negative responses (to say the least), so some of these women decided that the moment was right for an autonomous movement fighting for the liberation of women. It targeted patriarchal relations in the broader social world but also challenged the male-dominated movements of the day. Challenging movements for their exclusion and oppression was of course not invented in the 1960s. You only need to look at earlier histories of Black challenges to white-dominated movements in the United States[44] or at the ways in which resistance to the British Empire in the territories it colonized shaped anti-colonial dissent within Britain itself.[45] There are also countless examples in the last fifty years of North American social movements facing collective challenge from their own members and from other movements to broaden their approaches to justice and liberation. Relations of challenge are an important part of the work to strengthen such struggles.

Overall, there is no simple, singular lesson waiting to be derived from the ideas about movements I present in this chapter and in particular from this central role that the work of listening to the world and to each other plays in struggles for social justice and collective liberation. But it does perhaps point to a sensibility for approaching our engagement with movements. It suggests a role for thinking in terms of relations and responsiveness, for cultivating an attunement to our own listening and to how others might be listening. It suggests that we might benefit if more of us were to envision movement politics not just in the realm of abstract ideas about power and injustice but in the complicated everyday mess of how we are already connected, how we might connect differently, and what we might do together.

chapter 8

learning from movements

As we have seen over the course of this book, listening is not just something that each of us does at the individual level. It is also integral to how the social world is woven and to our struggles to change it. That more expansive and social understanding of listening is important and useful in itself, but it also offers opportunities for thinking differently about listening at the scale at which we conventionally conceive it — that is, as a practice we engage in as individuals.

At the most basic level, the popular listening advice we sampled earlier in the book is often premised on a limited understanding of what listening is, and approaching such advice with a richer understanding has the potential to make it more useful. Most of the ways such sources tell us to improve our listening suggest a much greater capacity for us to intervene deliberately and consciously in modifying the diverse cluster of practices that together we label "listening" than is the case. When anxiety was impeding my listening at the school dance and the labour movement event, just telling myself to relax would have been, to say the least, ineffective. No one-time self-admonition to really want to learn or to try to perceive my own assumptions would have made much of a dent in my limited capacity to effectively listen to talk about race or about desire in my late teens. Deliberate effort in the moment can sometimes make a difference, of course, and there are more sophisticated versions of this kind of advice that tell us to make changes to our listening not through effort in a single moment but via ongoing, recursive self-fashioning, and that can be useful too. But we cannot avoid the fact that our listening practices are the sedimented outcome of a lifetime of experiences and that changing them through deliberate, conscious effort, while not impossible, is usually neither easy nor quick.

There is further value to approaching listening with a clearer understanding not only of listening as a stubbornly stable assemblage of practices that we as individuals enact but of the social character of the world and how that shapes our listening and the landscape in which we do it. I can think of two kinds of resources — both part of a general category we'll talk about in a minute — that take analyses of the social world related to power and collective struggle (though often at a greater or lesser remove from the latter) and articulate ideas that can be read as listening advice even though they are not necessarily framed as such.

The first is writing informed by anti-racism/anti-oppression politics that does political education targeting largely (though in some cases not only) people who benefit from one or more axes of oppression — so, books for men to learn about sexism, for white people to learn about racism, and so on.[1] The general idea with such books is that they take analyses of the social world that have emerged from struggle and/or from scholarly work that is itself downstream from insights that came out of struggle, articulate them in a lay-oriented way that is pitched to be useful for the particular audience the book aims to educate, and combine that with suggestions about what readers can do. The exact tone and balance vary from instance to instance, but there is often at least a brief explicit consideration of listening. In the anti-racism books, the importance of white people listening to Black, Indigenous, and racialized peoples is usually articulated at least in passing. The bulk of content in these books is not framed in terms of listening, but it is nonetheless about listening as I understand it, in that they are working to get those who benefit from some axis of harm to be more responsive to the realities, voices, and struggles of those who experience that harm. Some of these books do a lot of translation for the benefit of their target audience to ease that listening process by providing a synthesis or summary of key research, writing, and commonly articulated arguments and perhaps spelling out common impediments to the ways of acting in the world they are trying to cultivate.

This genre of book has been subject to lots of critique. Some of that is from sources that are interested in defending the unjust status quo, but some is from perspectives supportive of social justice and collective liberation. There is lots of variation within this genre, so not all such books have the same limitations. Some of them have been a way that privileged individuals have built lucrative careers talking about axes of oppression they do not themselves experience, in ways that take space and opportunities from activists/authors/consultants who do experience that harm. Other critics argue that a focus on being palatable for privileged readers means that more transformative ideas and implications are easily lost. In concentrating attention on individual change by privileged people rather than collective struggle by oppressed people, such books can convey a distorted understanding of how change happens (even though they do often contain at least a nod to collective struggle). Such books are also at least sometimes taken up as part of larger processes in ways that are troubling. Some privileged people tend to respond to moments of heightened social movement momentum like the racial justice uprising of 2020 by reading books but not doing anything that might contribute directly to efforts on the ground. Or, far too often, such books are used as part of internal change initiatives by powerful institutions that convey the appearance of taking oppression seriously while, by design, accomplishing little or nothing of substance.

The other category of writing that isn't really listening advice but that can be read as such is some scholarly work. While a subset might explicitly use the language of listening, much more talks in terms of how we read/listen to texts, of how we can learn things about the social world, or of epistemology. It can be embedded in work situated across a wide range of themes, fields, and focuses. But you can read it all as listening advice. I am not going to attempt even a cursory survey of what is out there in those categories — this section notwithstanding, this book is still not a listening how-to — but I explore a couple of examples to get at the kinds of things such work can contain.

One seemingly common approach in scholarly sources feels like an extension of the more conventional listening advice focused on the receptivity and uptake of the person doing the listening but does so with greater attention to how we are socially produced subjects engaging in listening in a socially organized world. Take the idea of "vulnerable reading" or "vulnerable listening" from English and gender studies scholar Julietta Singh, who argues for

> listening as a critical mode of becoming vulnerable to the voices — human and nonhuman, audible and muted — that are always sounding even when we have not been trained or allowed ourselves to listen. ... Listening, as an act that might let each other in — psychically, physically — to another's ways of inhabiting the world.[2]

Among other things, such listening aims not so much for the acquisition of flat facts across difference but to construct a complex, nuanced, and sensitive "sympathetic imagination"[3] as we engage with other beings and the world — it presumes that those to whom we are listening are as complex and deserving of sympathy and compassion as we ourselves and uses our imaginative faculties to build our sense of them accordingly. It also requires a recognition that such sympathetic imagination inevitably comes to a point where it fails, that relating ethically to Others ultimately requires not more perfect knowing, however sympathetic in intention and complex in execution, but a constant return to asking and listening. It requires that we take up what we hear and see not only with reference to what is out there but to understanding the many and complex ways we ourselves are implicated and complicit in the oppression of others. It is deliberately seeking out that in the stories of others which can destabilize certainties in ourselves, particularly those bound up with (produced by, reproducing) oppressive power. "Vulnerable reading rewrites me."[4] Such listening is in part about knowing, but not knowing that gives power over, rather listening focused on being with: "We must press on listening to those voices that appear voiceless in order to produce new forms of engaged entanglement with and beyond ourselves."[5]

This is dense stuff, and what it means in practice is not immediately obvious. One critique of these types of sources, in fact, is that they can be too distant from everyday life and from common-sense understandings of the world for most of us to be able to derive much use from them. What they say about listening rarely takes the form of recipe-like steps but rather of insights into complex processes in a complex world applied to individual practice that are only as useful as our willingness and capacity to take them up, wrestle with their practical implications in an ongoing way, and deploy our partial and ever-evolving understandings in the course of our cyclical journeys of listening and knowing. They do not point to simple answers but to the possibility of shifting gradually over time to a different way of being and doing in the world than the one with which we began but in ways that are hard to foresee. It is precisely this engagement with complexity and with power that makes such scholarly writing potentially useful — it offers hints, though not easy ones, about how we might orient ourselves to doing those things, given the world that made us and that we inhabit.

Another broad approach found in scholarly sources engages even more directly with the socially organized character of the world. When read with listening explicitly in mind, these sources suggest that we re-think listening and knowing practices in ways that take their situated character into account. That is, they help us deepen our understanding of how we are socially positioned, now and over time, and how that shapes our capacities and practices for listening, which can be important to further developing those capacities and practices.

Dylan Robinson is a Stó:lō writer and scholar. He draws on Stó:lō thought to identify "settler colonial forms of perception," characterized by "a settler's starving orientation," as "hungry listening."[6] In line with the analyses of colonial listening and knowing discussed earlier, hungry listening is a rapacious, consumptive, extractive way of relating to the world, one that marks how settlers and our institutions often relate to Indigenous Peoples and their lands, and also a more general settler way of being. It is a logic that informs our listening and so much else. Despite emerging from a specific history and set of relations, Robinson argues that it shapes dominant listening practices more generally. Part of what he recommends we do in response has to do with developing practices that refuse hungry listening's urgent pace and consumptive premise:

> Hungry listening consumes without awareness of how the consumption acts in relationship with those people, the lands, the waters who provide sustenance. Moving beyond hungry listening toward anti-colonial listening practices requires that the "fevered" pace of consumption for knowledge resources be placed aside in favor of new temporalities of wonder disoriented from antirelational and nonsituated settler colonial positions of certainty.[7]

Another crucial element of what he calls for is listening grounded in consciousness of what he describes as "critical listening positionality,"[8] an idea that seems analogous to standpoint but deployed specifically to enhance listening. Robinson says that it "involves a self-reflexive questioning of how race, class, gender, sexuality, ability, and cultural background intersect and influence the way we are able to hear sound, music, and the world around us."[9] It involves actively engaging with how we have learned to listen and to know through how we have been formed as subjects due to our experiences of our social positionality and our socially organized relations with others. Robinson states: "As part of our listening positionality, we each carry listening privilege, listening biases, and listening ability that are never wholly positive or negative; by becoming aware of normative listening habits and abilities, we are better able to listen otherwise."[10] He argues that "positionality's importance derives not from its prevalent use as confession or admission of guilt. Instead, its usefulness is predicated upon … understanding positionality not as a static construct, but as a process or state that fundamentally guides our actions and perception."[11]

As with Singh's work, there is no clear set of instructions about how to do this. No magic answer is promised, contra so much listening advice of the more popular sort. Rather, Robinson offers perceptive analysis of features of self and of the world that we must attend to, take up, and make our own meaning from, in order to improve our listening in incremental ways as we move through our messy, recursive journey. There are also many other scholars — many of whom, unlike these two, do not use the word "listening" — whose work can be similarly read not for clear solutions to our failures of listening but for, again, complex insights into our complex world that can inform our ongoing efforts to listen and learn.

listening to everyday and movement struggle

Lay-oriented anti-racism/anti-oppression resources and the subset of scholarly sources that I think have the most potential to be useful exist as a result of both everyday and movement struggles for justice and liberation. They might be somewhat or even substantively distant from such struggles, but they are at least to some degree informed by them, shaped by them, downstream from them. In fact, this relationship to struggle is an important part of whatever is useful and powerful in such sources. With that in mind, there is value to thinking through listening practices with an even more direct focus on what social movements and communities-in-struggle have to offer. A central part of not just knowing the world but knowing it better, of listening in a way that takes into account what we know about how the social world is organized, and of listening and knowing in a way oriented towards social justice and collective liberation, must be listening directly to people who are engaged in struggles to make those sorts of changes. This means listening to the words they say aloud, to what they draw and sing and sign, to the ways they take action, to what they write. This starts from a recognition that the socially organized differentiation of listening practices related to standpoint is not just a product of differences in experience in some passive sense but is at least partially a result of active engagement with the world. We don't just float down the river of life and get buffeted by different currents and turn out differently as a result. As we are carried down that river, we *do* things, and the world reacts to what we do. From those actions and reactions, we learn and are further shaped.

Back in the 1960s, there was a sociologist called Harold Garfinkel who came up with an approach called ethnomethodology.[12] Its goal was to learn about how people's actions produce the everyday contexts in which we exist and how people make sense of such contexts. As is always true of things academic there is a lot more to it than this, but part of what it involved was having people go out and do things in everyday settings that were outside of the normative expectations for those settings. Breaching experiments, he called these — you do something weird around unexpecting people, and you see what they do in response. Those reactions would be a source of information, a basis for producing knowledge about how those situations were organized and understood by the people in them.

In everyday situations of oppression, the decision to engage in everyday resistance (and perhaps some other ways of asserting dignity as well) can be understood as analogous to a breaching experiment. Dominant norms generally dictate compliance and a kind of submersion of self in the dominant story of what is happening. By definition, everyday resistance and the assertion of dignity are refusals of that norm. Of course it is not quite the same, because the breaches engineered by Garfinkel and his collaborators were done precisely to evoke a response in order to learn about the context, while everyday resistance is often calibrated to avoid or minimize serious consequences. Certainly, knowledge production is not the main point of everyday resistance but rather an unintended and probably often unconscious side effect. Nonetheless, even acting in ways meant to be hidden or in ways meant to avoid a harsh response employs knowledge about how oppressive circumstances are put together — how else would you know what to do? — and putting that knowledge to use tests it and develops it further starting from how the other people in that situation respond, or don't. It is therefore arguable that moments of everyday resistance are particularly rich contexts for learning about our unjust world. People subject to a particular oppression learn things about it in an everyday way precisely through the fraught, ongoing pressure of actively living in dignity and perhaps resisting in the face of circumstances that punish those things.

When you move from considering everyday resistance to more deliberately collective and self-consciously political resistance, the dynamics are analogous. Collective struggle is intrinsically a place where knowledge production happens and also a process which drives knowledge production.[13] If you want to get a stop sign at the end of your street, it is not good enough just to wish for it, and it is not even good enough just to get your neighbours together. You need to know who makes that decision. You need to know both your own reasons for wanting the sign and also the kinds of arguments and actions that your neighbours and your city council might respond to. You need to know about different ways that community groups can exert pressure. As we touched on earlier, one type of work involved in collectively fighting for change involves producing knowledge (doing research) to inform your demands and your campaign.

In some kinds of movements and some contexts, this research might be recognized as such, and people with specialized skills might put considerable effort into doing it and using it to produce a report, a policy document, or something similar.[14] Sometimes it is even done by academics in university-based settings, though it is worth being cautious about scholars who are doing research related to social movements — too often that ends up meaning research that is *about* but not particularly *useful to* social movements.[15] The research that happens within movements may not feel like research at all, and those engaged in it may not think of it in that way, but it is, nonetheless, work that involves deliberately listening to the world in order to generate knowledge.

This research, wherever it is done, can be what you might call tactical — it is about the nuts and bolts of what you face, to inform your action; and it can be political — understanding the issue and marshalling your arguments so that even if there is no hope of convincing whatever uncaring violent institution you face, you can use them to mobilize more of your neighbours. Similar kinds of things are true in any struggle. You want to get your university to stop investing in fossil fuel industries?[16] As you organize to do that, you will no doubt end up learning a bunch about how your university works, about investing, and about the fossil fuel industry. Your health system has a policy that is unjust towards Indigenous children living in the North?[17] There are all kinds of things about how other health systems work, about medical best practices, about how this connects to larger histories of colonization and genocide, about pressure points in the health system and the provincial government, and lots more that can help you put together a response that might lead to overturning the policy.

However, it is not just a matter of figuring out what you need to know tactically and politically, doing the work to learn those things, and then engaging in action. Rather, the action itself is central to learning about the world, and there is an ongoing cycle in which action, reflection on that action, and other forms of research — sometimes this cycle of theory and action gets called praxis — are constantly feeding into each other. Or, at least, that *can* be true — it is all too easy to engage in action without the kind of attention and listening necessary to inform reflection and to guide future action.

When you engage in collective action, other people in their various socially organized contexts react, and you learn from that. There is, for one thing, a broader political learning that takes place — you hear responses and accounts and stories from a range of sources and perspectives, and careful attention to them can tell you a lot about the context and the politics of the situation. But a crucial part of the learning that comes from action is much more directly tied to the practical responses of the powerful institutions involved. What do those institutions do and how do they do it? Direct action — action that seeks to materially interfere in the activities of some powerful institution or arm of the state — can be particularly effective in evoking the kinds of responses that give this knowledge.[18] When activists engaging in mass direct action are arrested and put in jail, what does that allow them to learn in a practical, material sense about the carceral system?[19] When students occupy the office of a university administrator, what does the administration do and what can the students learn from that about how universities work and about how control over space is regulated?[20] In other words, action — especially but not only direct action — can give insights into and/or can be a powerful starting point for investigating how institutions relevant to the struggle in question are socially organized, which can be crucial information for winning.

An important classic paper that captured this dynamic was "Political Activist as Ethnographer" by Canadian sociologist George Smith.[21] He was a student of (and unrelated to) Dorothy Smith, whose work we briefly discussed earlier. He was involved in the organizing in response to the police raids on gay bathhouses in Toronto in the early 1980s and in the early stages of organizing in response to the HIV/AIDS epidemic later that decade. In addition to being an activist, he brought his capacities as a sociologist to bear and through that work developed considerable insight into using "political confrontation as an ethnographic resource."[22] He outlines an approach that, building on his mentor's work, begins from the moment of confrontation or rupture and then proceeds to ask practical questions about what happened and about how and why it happened that way. For instance, it was initially common among the gay men active in the organizing in response to the bathhouse raids to blame the raids on the homophobia of low-ranking police officers or electoral maneuvering by the provincial Conservative Party. While no doubt there was no shortage of personal anti-queer sentiment among the cops involved in the raids and one can never discount the kinds of shenanigans that a political party will use to retain power, by a rigorous yet practical exploration of what exactly the police did and how, Smith was able to clarify the ways in which aspects of the Criminal Code were being mobilized to police the sexualities of gay and bisexual men, which in turn could be used to inform the decisions by organizers about political goals and ways to pursue them.

There are different ways to go about doing that learning. Certainly, many movements could benefit from deliberately applying the methods of George Smith's "political activist ethnography."[23] But even when there is not the same kind of approach brought to the work that a movement-embedded radical sociologist might apply, there is still plenty of learning in and by movements for exactly the same practical reasons that everyday resistance both requires and results in understanding of the circumstances in which it is happening — activists and organizers want to win, and they want to avoid punitive consequences, so they are attuned to what happens when they act.

The knowledge that movements produce is not only useful for the movements that produce it but can also be valuable to the rest of us. The late Aziz Choudry, a long-time activist and radical scholar who worked in Montreal and Johannesburg and who wrote extensively on research and learning in social movements, repeatedly makes the point that scholars whose work in some way relates to social movements often do not pay enough attention to the knowledge generated by those movements themselves in the course of struggle.[24] Perhaps more importantly, he argues that the rest of us should pay attention to that knowledge too: "Communities, movements, and people around the world can learn from and build upon the powerful insights that emerge out of past and present movements for change."[25]

While listening to what others have learned about the world during individual and collective struggles can be an important resource, particularly when we don't share those struggles, we also need to figure out how to assess what we hear.

evaluating what we hear from movements

To a large extent, listening to people talk about what they have learned in the course of struggle and then making knowledge from that yourself is much like any other kind of listening and learning. But there are also a few potential pressures specific to it that are worth mentioning. One such pressure tells us to flat-out dismiss knowledge produced in struggle. This is, after all, what we see modelled by many powerful institutions and in most mainstream discourse — silent, invisible erasure, or token acknowledgement and immediate rejection. Another impulse that people sometimes experience is the exact opposite, often as a reaction against the pressure to dismiss — that is, to take knowledge produced in individual or collective struggle up with no critical evaluation at all. This can be a response to being overwhelmed by the novelty of it and just not having any basis to evaluate what we are hearing. Or it can be a deliberate gesture of political support to renounce our own critical faculties when faced with the words of a particular person, group, or movement. While well-intentioned, this is misguided and is at heart just a different kind of disrespect for those to whom we are listening. As we have seen, understanding the world is complex, and inevitably situated and imperfect, and no single account will ever do everything that we need, so we have to take it *all* up critically. Additionally, there are always differences within and between movements, within and between communities-in-struggle, related to aspects of experience, analysis, and politics, to the inherent complexity of the world, and to the difficult and fraught character of the work of trying to understand and change it. It is perhaps even subtly dehumanizing to not recognize that everyone to whom we are listening as we learn about the world has to deal with all that.

Let's face it, in movements there are pressures to make good knowledge because people in movements want to win, but there is still plenty of opportunity to engage in ideological mystification, to take up distortion from the broader culture or from other specific sources, or to just get things wrong. I have observed multiple times already that the world is complex and humans are fallible, and that is just as relevant to knowledge production in movements. We can look again at George Smith's account of the hard and determined work it took to displace cop homophobia and Conservative skullduggery as dominant accounts within the movement of the origin of the bathhouse raids with a more grounded understanding. Or you can easily imagine a situation where, say, a group of tenants is working from a mix of grounded practical knowledge of the struggle against predatory landlords, keen insights into broader questions of housing, capitalism, and discrimination that mainstream commentators ignore, *and also* political narratives about the situation that further investigation or experience of struggle in a new direction would demonstrate are just not accurate.

Moreover, as we have already talked about, the same kinds of oppressive power that silence, erase, and marginalize in the social world as a whole are sometimes reproduced within social movements and communities-in-struggle. These "tensions and exclusions related to race, gender, and class" within movements, Choudry says, have "implications ... for the claims made by movements and activists and the resulting nature of the knowledge produced in and about these struggles."[26] He writes that, in more than a few instances, "more radical ideas are silenced, erased, contained, or watered down, and tensions and contradictions glossed over."[27] So all the same questions we would ask in any other context about who is present and who is absent, who is speaking and who has been silenced, who is centred and who is made marginal, need to be asked when we are listening to accounts of the world produced in struggle, and doing so is a crucial form of critical engagement.

A third impulse that comes up when we are listening to knowledge produced in everyday and movement struggles relates to what many of us have learned about what it means to engage critically. In the late 1990s, queer theorist Eve Kosofsky Sedgwick wrote about the idea of "paranoid reading," which I think can equally be understood as "paranoid listening," as the dominant mode of critical engagement in queer studies and in critical theory in general.[28] I first encountered the term in an article by radical activist and writer Chris Dixon in the wonderful grassroots magazine *Briarpatch*, and he, in turn, had heard it applied this way in movement contexts from two grad student activists in Victoria, BC, named Kim Smith and Nick Montgomery.[29] They describe paranoid reading as "a way of relating with people, ideas, and activities by looking primarily for their failures and limitations; it's about criticizing first and asking questions later, if at all," and they suggest it "has become the dominant mode of engagement on the radical left."

I suspect that the idea that this is what it means to relate critically to what we hear and see and read is partly responsible for the impulse to reject critical engagement entirely — if our only model for doing it is harsh, disrespectful, and focused purely on fault, then refusing critical engagement with people we want to support out of a sense of political responsibility becomes more comprehensible. But there are many ways to engage critically, and many of them are both more focused on building than tearing down and more respectful of those to whom we are listening. Indeed, critical engagement can be a form of actively valuing and honouring the ideas of those with whom we engage. Sedgwick argues for treating "paranoid reading" as one approach among many and suggests exploring the possibilities for what she calls "reparative reading," which can be just as legitimate as part of building our knowledge in a violent, oppressive world. Dixon quotes Smith and Montgomery as recommending the cultivation of "kindness, curiosity, gratitude, and other ways of relating [that] can come to seem naive or counter-productive when paranoia is the reflex." You could also characterize this as deliberately trying to enact listening practices that are generous — not uncritical, certainly not forgiving of dehumanization or anything like that, but setting aside much of the impulse to dismiss and deliberately countering how we undermine our own "capacity to be curious, open, and vulnerable."[30]

kinds of movement knowledge

It can also be important to relate to the different kinds of knowledge that get produced in the course of struggle in different ways. As discussed earlier, some of that knowledge is grounded, practical, experience-level understanding of how nearby elements of the social world are put together, as discovered through everyday resistance, collective direct action, and other kinds of activities. While it is just as important to relate to this kind of knowledge critically-yet-generously as any other, its direct connection to the practical and the experiential mean that it has the potential, at least, for a robustness that is not necessarily true of other kinds of knowledge — it is a direct product of intervening and observing, of a built-in empirical testing that stays close to the level of life as we actually live it. As such, it has the potential to be used in much the way I talked about using experience in evaluating accounts of the social world, as a testing and grounding for them. If your theory says X about the police, but in blocking a bridge or sitting in at an MP's office your friend has learned Y, it would be foolish of you to just hang onto X and dismiss Y.

Collective struggle produces lots of other knowledge that begins from a clear and direct grounding in that experience but reaches beyond it in necessarily less grounded ways. Movements and their participants tend to start from those experiences but, as is true of all of us, have to listen to, evaluate, and learn from other sources in order to generate accounts of the social world and other analyses with a broader sweep and reach. When they do so, what they produce tends to explain the world in ways that take their own experiences seriously, which dominant accounts often do not. Listening deeply and openly to such analyses is a critical element of listening to knowledge produced in struggle. Choudry points out that it is not unusual for those outside of a given social context or struggle to fixate on what oppressed and exploited people say about their *experiences* while failing to recognize the power of the *analyses* of the world, of what needs to change, and of how change needs to happen that they also produce.[31]

Another form of knowledge that we hear from those engaged in everyday and movement struggles is stories. In fact, this is probably what we encounter the most often. Some would even argue that pretty much everything we hear and read is packaged as a story, even when we don't recognize it as such, including the broad accounts of the social world just discussed. For many thinkers, this is a problem. Some scoff at stories as an inferior mechanism for conveying the supposed hard facts those thinkers valorize. Others argue that stories entrap us irretrievably in dominant ideologies. Shari Stone-Mediatore, though, argues that this ubiquity of stories is not a bad thing at all — we just need better ways of responsibly evaluating them.[32]

There are a few different kinds of things that we can get from stories. We *can* get what you might conventionally describe as facts — straightforward, empirically verifiable claims about material aspects of the world. We should be careful about that — there was a tendency among early enthusiasts for oral history and "history from below" to relate to people's stories as only and always factual accounts, when we should know even from how we ourselves tell stories about our own lives that it is seldom that simple. Memory is fallible and partial, as are even our most careful approaches to narrativizing our own experiences. As well, the supposedly straightforward character of what counts as fact, and the contents thereof, can be deceptive — an outcome of socially produced dominant common sense that falls apart under the right kind of scrutiny — so it is not necessarily easy to unambiguously extract "fact" from story. But, still, dealt with carefully, stories can be one part of building that kind of knowledge.

But Stone-Mediatore argues that this is only one element, and a relatively minor one, of the value and power of stories in our public life. They are not just conveyances of fact, but an imaginative synthesis of a complex whole that reflects the teller's situated self, values, and analyses — which are exactly the sorts of things built up by the sedimentation of their journey of experience, action, and reflection through a socially organized world. This is not just about the total of propositional statements in a story but the complex whole constructed through every rhetorical and narrative element. To return once more to George Smith's example, the initial accounts of many of the gay men organizing against the bathhouse raids may not have captured grounded knowledge useful for orienting resistance — that required something else. But in speculating about the anti-queer actions of police officers and Conservative Party officials, they *were* conveying important knowledge about their lives and about Ontario in the early 1980s. Even when not every detail is accurate or evaluable, the complex whole of stories can still carry valuable and powerful knowledge about the social world.

We need to have ways to assess stories, of course — how they are acting in the world, what we can learn from them, and so on. We must be able to identify and refuse the obviously violent, deceptive fantasies propagated by those actively working for a less just world. Because stories are often less linear, more complex sources of insight into the world, we need ways of deciding how to take them up and make meaning from them that are more sophisticated than trying to assess the truth value of individual, isolated claims.

One technique that Stone-Mediatore suggests — she calls it "enlarged thought," after the idea from Immanuel Kant that she adapts it from — is, as a listener, engaging with the stories you hear by taking up other standpoints, particularly marginalized standpoints. When you hear a story about the polity currently called "Canada," it is a useful initial practice for non-Indigenous people to say, how might Indigenous people take up and react to this story? There is never a unitary or simple answer to that, and those of us who are not Indigenous cannot answer that definitively, but starting from that question can be a powerful way to begin assessing that, say, this story that denies the harms of residential schools is not, in fact, a useful story to use in understanding the world. Stone-Mediatore writes that doing this is in part an imaginative act, a placing of yourself in the shoes of another, an act of perspective-taking. But she also stresses that it cannot be purely imaginative, or it is doomed to failure. Rather, it must be a product of ongoing and sustained material engagement with what people who live that standpoint have to say about the world, themselves, and the issues in question. At the same time, doing this is not just substituting someone else's judgement for your own, for all the reasons that we cannot renounce critical engagement when we listen to others. You are still assessing the story as *you*, and not pretending otherwise, and perspective-taking is just a means to do that. It is a way to begin to understand what the story in question is doing in the world, what is missing from its account, how the story itself engages with standpoints other than the one it is told from, and so on.

Stone-Mediatore suggests a number of other things that we should be mindful of as well, both as we tell stories and as we take up stories told by others.[33] This is not how she frames them, but at least some of them seem to boil down to taking seriously and engaging honestly with features of how the social world is organized and of how we know the world, as discussed in earlier pages of this book. Does the story you are listening to reflect the inevitable complexity of the world, or is it told in ways that erase and avoid it? She also suggests thinking about how a story makes efforts (or not) to be "communicable." This captures not just the obvious elements of anticipating how your audience might be listening, such as the accessibility of its language, but communicability in a broader sense, including how it relates, in the ways that it is told, to the reality that the listeners/readers who will be taking it up will hold a range of standpoints, understandings, and accounts of the world. How does the story reflect the fact that how we know the world is inevitably partial, situated, and incomplete? How does it reflect the unavoidable limits in our capacity to understand perspectives fundamentally different from our own and to incorporate that awareness into our narratives of self and world? How does it push back against what she describes as "community-wide prejudice" — which I take to mean harmful distortions of knowing baked, in a collective way, into our language, our listening practices, and our social organization? In other words, unjust power organizes our world and therefore our stories of the world and how we take them up, so how does this story challenge or undermine that?

 This is a lot, and as you will no doubt not be surprised to hear, I raise it to point towards the kinds of things we need to think about, rather than in the service of trying to produce a rigid methodology for telling and assessing stories. But I do think one more point from Stone-Mediatore is worth taking seriously. She emphasizes the importance of listening to what she describes as "marginal experience narratives" — a formulation not identical to but overlapping with what I am talking about as stories of everyday and movement struggle — as valuable resources for learning about the world, precisely because they often do a lot of these things. Yes, as some scholars insist, such stories (as is true of all stories) cannot escape the dominant ideologies of the world that are embedded into the very language and other narrative resources that are our only way to tell stories and the social world that shapes both that and our listening practices. But even so, through how they are oriented to dominant narratives and through the mechanisms of their telling, they draw attention to tensions, contradictions, other ways of listening and knowing. They draw attention to power, to challenges and struggles, to hints at a better world. Though they are always situated and partial, they are not subsumed by dominant ideologies but rather exist within, against, and perhaps beyond them.

the limits remain

Clearly, many ways of engaging with what people say about what they face in their everyday lives, with what movements and communities-in-struggle say, and with other kinds of knowledge that derive from all of that can help us understand the social world and can contribute to our journeys of developing richer and more sophisticated listening practices. But what does that mean, what can it do, in the face of the socially produced limits of listening discussed earlier in the book? As important as it can be to develop our listening in these directions, what can we really do in the face of the weight of the last five centuries of history and how that shapes our possibilities for listening today?

CONCLUSION

listening shapes movements, movements shape listening

The questions at the end of the last chapter point in some pretty bleak directions. Even setting aside whatever hard limits there might be related to the laws of physics, to the complexity of the world, and to human fallibility, the socially produced pressures towards failures of listening tower over any steps we might take in our own listening journeys. We cannot individually listen our way out of the last five centuries of history and how they have shaped us, our world, and our listening in the present, no matter how devotedly we listen to movements or how carefully we take up relevant insights from critical scholars.

This could be, I suppose, a set-up for exhorting us all to accept the inevitability of human limitations and the need to make our peace with them. Certainly, there are some instances, some failures of listening, where that is not a bad idea. There will always, sadly, be the kinds of failures of listening that mean an encounter at a school dance results in hurt feelings.[1] But the harms and injustices of listening that are socially produced — those we cannot be content with, those we cannot accept as inevitable. What I want to leave you with is the suggestion that we do not have to. We do not have to regard socially produced failures of listening as a permanent feature of our lives, even given the serious limits to what we can do as individuals, any more than we have to accept any of the other outcomes of the violent, harmful, unjust way that our world is socially organized.

I talk lots in this book about the role of listening in weaving the world and about all the ways listening is at work in our efforts to change it. But this relationship goes in the other direction as well — collective struggle and the social transformation it can lead to are the only way we will create the conditions that will allow us to listen more effectively and more justly. This means a few different things. Some of the thinkers mentioned earlier who have described the profoundly colonial/imperial character of dominant listening practices have been part of collective efforts to develop new approaches to knowing (listening to) the world that push back against socially imposed failures of listening in a way that no individual effort ever could. These efforts include scholarship but also exploring and making meaning from the world in creative, imaginative, and artistic ways emerging from lives and standpoints that face the worst of this world's violence. Such efforts are important in their own right. They can also be understood as one facet of broader collective struggles that take more direct and overtly political forms. Not only are such struggles the only thing that have ever won meaningful change in the many forms of social organization that oppress and exploit, but those struggles and the transformation they promise hold the potential to reconfigure our social relations in ways that would allow for listening that is, in every sense, better.

It is not obvious from where we stand now what the resulting world might look like, either in general or when it comes to our horizons of possibility for listening to each other and to the world. As always, if someone promises you a rigid blueprint in advance, they are lying. But, still, we can imagine the broad outlines. It is a world in which the land has been given back and is no longer treated as property, a world in which Black lives really do matter, a world in which Palestine is free, a world not pervaded by sexual assault, a world with no billionaires and no homelessness, a world freed of the relentlessly consumptive drive of capital, a world in which the violence that is borders has been abolished and no one is illegal, a world in which gender and sexuality are sites of self-realization and play rather than constraint and harm, a world in which we work together to shape our lives rather than having their shape violently imposed. It is also a world in which we are not deprived of the practices we need to listen well and meaningfully to the people around us, people across town, and people on the other side of the world.

This is in part about listening that is more effective — listening that is not twisted away from an accurate reflection of the world by centuries of oppressive social relations. It is also about listening that is more just. So, to go back to an idea we talked about earlier, this will not be a world in which transparency — the drive to unbounded, dominating knowing that Édouard Glissant argues is so central to Western cultural logics — is taken to ever-greater extremes. Part of a world built on relations that are respectful of the dignity, autonomy, and agency of those for whom such things are so often violated today is the right not to be known, the right to refuse transparency. In place of the drive to listen and see and know all, which is also the reduction of the richness of the world into categories suitable for ruling, there must be space, especially for those who are today subject to dominating scrutiny, to not be seen, not be heard, not be known. "Opacity," Glissant calls this.[2] "The right to be unseen and unseeable," nehiyaw poet and scholar Billy-Ray Belcourt defines it.[3] "Refusal," is what Kanyen'kehà:ka anthropologist Audra Simpson names something very similar.[4]

This opacity is not separation, not a refusal of the world, but a refusal of dominating listening and knowing. It is an acceptance of limitations on the reach of our listening in the service of making it more just. It is how listening will work in a world in which we know that we don't know everything about each other, but what we do know is no longer corrupted by oppressive histories and by the imperatives of transparency and ruling. As Glissant says, "We clamor for the right to opacity for everyone."[5] He scoffs at "windbags [who] are anxiously intent on confining themselves to the false transparency of a world they used to run; they do not want to enter into the penetrable opacity of a world in which one exists, or agrees to exist, with and among others."[6] He writes:

> I thus am able to conceive of the opacity of the other for me, without reproach for my opacity for him. To feel in solidarity with him or to build with him or to like what he does, it is not necessary for me to grasp him. It is not necessary to try to become the other (to become other) nor to "make" him in my image.[7]

This is not an easy path, nor a quick one, and what exactly we must do to reach such a world is just as unclear in this context as in any other. We must not yearn unrealistically for some magical moment of change just over the horizon. We must avoid the left fantasy of a singular apocalyptic event through which everything will be resolved. We must instead recognize that it will take lifetimes of complicated, uneven struggle.

This brings us back once again to the scream and the murmur. My listening is deeply imperfect and often fails, in terms of both effectiveness and justice, but even so I still often manage to hear the scream and the murmur, to see them, to taste them all around. I hear them enough to know that they are present, that they are everywhere. In sensing them, they push me to focus not on seeking individual perfection in the face of my failures as an individual listener but rather to ask what we can do together, based on these things we already see and hear and smell and taste and feel.

These, remember, are the sounds of survival and struggle and, sometimes, thriving. They are not conveyances of detail nor invitations, by themselves, to further listening. They mark, they signal, but they do not explore or explain. They point to irrepressible being, to selfhood, to persistence, to rage, to grief, to dignity, to joy, and ultimately to the world that is and the world that must be. Straining to listen well to the scream and the murmur is not about pursuit of information, of reconstructing the facts of the world. It is most definitely not about the kind of listening that fills categories of ruling, the kind that advances transparency, the kind that endlessly tries and fails to fill the belly of the hungry listener.

Rather, to listen to the scream and the murmur is to honour the survival, struggle, joy, and dignity they express — for ourselves, for those around us, for those across town and around the world. It is hearing, in our own voice and those of others, the horror and the hope, the rejection of the current world and the longing for a better one, however inchoate they might be. It is seeing dignity thrust in the face of its denial, dignity asserted despite its denial. It is sensing, in every way, selves calling out for justice and liberation. To listen to the murmur and the scream is to let the raw, pervasive fact of these things inform our actions. And then, collectively, doing something about it. This is the listening that is the starting point for any path to a better world — to any world that enables better listening, to the possibility of a responsiveness to each other that is effective and just.

epilogue

I breath slowly and deeply. Years after my first keystrokes about listening, I sit yet again facing my laptop in a quiet room on a quiet street, in a calm corner of the hubbub. I need to clear my head, so I put on boots, hat, and jacket, and walk out my front door. I debate going left to the big neighbourhood park or right towards the core of the downtown and opt for the latter. As I walk, I move past a scattering of other pedestrians and plenty of cars, as well as highrises, convenience stores, and the fenced site where a building burned down last year. I run into someone I know from years ago, and we engage in the ritual of the catch-up, awkward but warm. I put on my N95 mask — not many still do — to walk through the mall, stopping at the pharmacy to pick up a prescription renewal. Then I wander out the other side and into the little park right at the heart of the downtown. It's chilly, so I won't linger for too long, but I sit on a bench, watch the fountain, listen to the world flow around me, and also intermittently glance at my phone and take in voices from other whens and wheres.

In listening to the city, with only a little effort, I sense those same two figurative expressions of survival and living and struggle and thriving that are always there, wherever we are, whatever we are doing — the murmur and the scream. I listen to the two guys who are sitting on the next bench over. I try not to eavesdrop, but I can't avoid hearing fragments of conversation, jokes, gossip. I could be wrong — my middle-class senses might be misleading me — but based on their appearance and on things they say, they seem to be homeless, or at least what social service agencies euphemistically call "street-involved," and therefore living in deep poverty and (at best) precariously housed. What could be starker? There they are, on the sharp end of one of the harshest manifestations of socially produced violence, indignity, and harm — in recent years unhoused people in Canada have been targets of disgusting rhetoric by some politicians and homeowners and enthusiastic brutality from police, as well as targets of all of the systemic violence of social relations that push people into poverty, make housing unaffordable, cut and privatize the services they need, and prioritize policing and carceral responses over genuine support. Also, there they are, quietly asserting their dignity, enjoying the cool spring sun and some time with a friend.

I listen, and I think about listening. Even these many years later, after all the research and reflection that have gone into writing this book, I still have lots of questions about listening. Sure, some of those are the unresolvable ones about improving my own personal listening practices — I try to pay the necessary attention to those without letting them carry me away, sometimes successfully and sometimes not. But there are lots of other questions too. There is so much more I want to know about how the social world is organized and the ways in which our responsive capacities play a role in that. There is so much more to figure out about how listening to a world woven through listening allows us to know and about how our situatedness within the weave shapes our knowing. There is so much more to know about the roles that listening plays in movements and about the ways movements can enable better listening.

But as I sit on that cast iron bench — now kind of listening to passing cars and cooing pigeons and fragments of nearby conversation, but not really listening to any of that at all — I am mostly thinking about listening to the future. Like I said earlier, I think it is meaningful to talk about listening to the social world in ways that go at least a little beyond our immediate local vicinity, through the ways in which *more* reverberates down to us through the social relations that shape both the voices and the general sensory input that reach our eyes and ears, often enabled and amplified by our existing knowledge and sometimes also by deliberate investigation. Just as we can listen to that which is but is not nearby, we can in a similar but even more precarious and partial way listen to that which is not yet. Sometimes our sense of being able to do this is little more than us projecting our own fears and hopes. But we can also do it in ways that are at least a little more grounded than that — ways that make use of our knowledge of the social world as it is now, that imaginatively project what it might be in a year, or ten, or a hundred. This is fraught and uncertain and points not towards any single path but to a hazy range of possibilities. But this *is* a kind of listening that we regularly do. Often, or perhaps always, when we intervene to create change at the individual level or as part of a collective effort, not only are we listening to each other and the world in the present in many different ways, but we are also listening to the range of futures that our actions and the actions of others might create.[1] When you decide to go to a rally at city hall demanding that money be taken from the police budget to fund social services, you are quite likely listening to the harms that policing causes in the here and now, you are listening to the other people you are standing with on that day, and you are also listening to futures in which abolitionist interventions in public life have had a range of levels of success.

As I sit here and contemplate listening to the future, the ever-present rush of cars pushes me again (in an echo of the backyard listening described earlier) to think about the climate crisis. Corporate-funded and far-right deniers pretend otherwise, and liberal deniers claim to believe but don't act like it, but this listening reminds me that our current levels of fossil fuel extraction and consumption, and the colonial and capitalist social relations that drive them, are on a path to make our world much less habitable and thus cause incredible indignity, harm, and suffering. Indeed, this is already happening. The fact that this is so clearly perceptible, not just from the stream of hydrocarbon-burning vehicles ten feet behind me but from so much of life in the twenty-first century, is really nothing to do with my own listening capacities but a result of one of the most thorough collective efforts at listening to the future humanity has ever undertaken. Its message is clear. It is not inevitable, but with each terrifying warning from Indigenous Elders, from frontline communities, and from the Intergovernmental Panel on Climate Change and with all the ongoing climate-destructive actions by governments of all stripes, it seems clear which futures elites and powerful institutions have chosen to pursue, unless we are able to stop them.[2]

As I listen to the future, I also hear more of the same oppressive, predatory violence that reverberates down from centuries past. I'm not sure I know enough to meaningfully guess at the new forms such violence might take next year or next decade, but I clearly hear it echoing back from the years ahead. With a new far-right regime in power in the United States, attacks on justice, on the common good, and on the well-being of many groups of people have reached agonizing new heights in that country, and this is giving support and space to those already hard at work with similar oppressive goals in the rest of the world. Even before Trump took power, we were seeing things like the Israeli state enacting genocidal violence in Gaza with the full support of the liberal establishment in the West and ominous shifts in how state practices in countries like the US and the UK were relating to 2SLGBTQI+ people, especially trans people, to the extent that queer and trans advocates are increasingly describing this trajectory as "eliminationist."[3] Canada, of course, has its own long history of genocide and oppression and its own home-grown forces working to make everything so much worse. As I listen to the future, I hear a rising wave of both tragic harms and inspiring resistance, with uncertain outcomes. Echoing dynamics in many other places, I hear in Canada the ominous rumblings of a growing far right, both in its grassroots, anti-system orientation and reflected in the halls of power.[4]

It is hard to be optimistic when listening to the future. And yet, I know that, in a profound way — to use a widely circulated quote from Joe Strummer of The Clash — "the future is unwritten."[5] I know this from listening to the histories of many movements past and from thinking back to the many moments of surprise in which the unthinkable became real even just in my lifetime. The listening we do to the future is not pointless, not pure fantasy, but even at its most grounded, it has significant limitations. Often, change happens in a way that no one could have predicted. While that can take us to terrible places, it can also do the opposite. According to feminist writer Rebecca Solnit, hope for a better future "is an embrace of the essential unknowability of the world, of the breaks with the present, the surprises."[6]

From people I know personally and from the many I interviewed over the years, I know that there are lots of us who are not relating to that future, to any future, in passive ways. There are the unknown millions who are resisting in their everyday lives, there are the heavily oppressed communities who have always been resisting together, and there are new people each day finding their way into more deliberately collective and self-consciously political resistance. This doesn't always get reported in the news, and it doesn't always show up in easily recognizable ways on social media. There are false starts and failures, there are setbacks and defeats. But sometimes — not often enough, but sometimes — we win, in ways that illuminate possible paths to much bigger victories.[7] Sometimes, some shift or breakthrough, some new infusion of energy, some new tactic produces big wins in a short time, and suddenly you can see how all the quiet, seemingly fruitless work over years was laying necessary groundwork. Sometimes, even if the outcome is never the kind of complete and final revolutionary fairy tale that so often burns in left imaginations, we manage to move forward in a way that puts us further ahead in some substantive sense. Needs are met, indignity and harm are mitigated, and the landscape is shifted in our favour for future struggles.

I'm cold, so I get up off the bench and make my way home. I settle into the comfy armchair by the front window and get out my laptop again. I check my schedule — a climate rally, tomorrow. I'm not involved in this organizing, not part of the relationships reconfigured in a sustained way to make this and related actions happen. But I'll go and be one body among hundreds, one little piece of more transiently reconfigured relationships contributing in a small way to the collective momentum building to push us towards the more liveable futures I can faintly hear. Then on Sunday, I have an online meeting for the grassroots media project I am part of, a small piece of movement infrastructure doing what we can to support efforts that are working in so many ways towards social justice and collective liberation. None of this is very much — none of what any individual can do is very much. But it is through doing it with others that it might, if we are determined and lucky, have world-historic consequences.

Soon, I will do more journalling as I continue to figure out what my work life will look like in six months, in twelve months. It's an open question, given that *Talking Radical Radio*'s ten-year weekly run feels, despite the passage of time, like it just ended and given that this book will soon be out of my hands and circulating in the world. I don't know exactly what I will do, what form my work will take. But it will no doubt continue to have something to do with listening, particularly to the voices of other participants in social movements and communities-in-struggle.

Thank-you, again, for listening to me.

Notes

introduction

1 People with synesthesia of course have different experiences of the relationships between different senses.
2 John Holloway, *Change the World Without Taking Power, New Edition* (London: Pluto Press, 2005).
3 M.M. Bakhtin, *The Dialogic Imagination: Four Essays* (Austin: University of Texas Press, 2010).
4 "Ottawa, the Far-Right, and the State: Inside the Convoy Protests and the Unfolding Three Way Fight," *It's Going Down* (podcast), February 11, 2022, itsgoingdown.org/ottawa-the-far-right-and-the-state/; Scott Neigh, "Ottawa Residents Against the Convoy, and for Solidarity and Social Justice," *Talking Radical Radio* (podcast), April 19, 2022, talkingradical.ca/2022/04/19/radio-ottawa-residents-against-the-convoy-and-for-solidarity-and-social-justice/; Scott Neigh, "Seeking Healing, Justice, and Change in the Wake of the Convoy Occupation," *Talking Radical Radio* (podcast), November 8, 2022, talkingradical.ca/2022/11/08/radio-seeking-healing-justice-and-change-in-the-wake-of-the-convoy-occupation/.
5 Admittedly, there probably are instances where the question of what to do with this commitment is a bit ambiguous, as our left movements past and present have never been perfect and exist within and against (a formulation I came to through the work of John Holloway) the social relations that produce all of this indignity and harm, rather than outside of them.
6 Thanks, Randy!
7 See talkingradical.ca for more information on both the original oral history project and *Talking Radical Radio*.
8 Scott Neigh, *Gender and Sexuality: Canadian History Through the Stories of Activists* (Halifax and Winnipeg: Fernwood Publishing, 2012); Scott Neigh, *Resisting the State: Canadian History Through the Stories of Activists* (Halifax and Winnipeg: Fernwood Publishing, 2012).
9 Scott Neigh, "Reflections Based on 10 Years of Talking Radical Radio," *Talking Radical,* April 19, 2023, talkingradical.ca/2023/04/19/reflections-based-on-10-years-of-talking-radical-radio/.
10 At some points in this book, I reference episodes of the show. Because of citation conventions, these appear under my name, but in doing this I am not referring you to my own words but rather to those of the activists, organizers, artists, thinkers, or other change-makers that I interviewed in the episode in question.

11 See, for example, Martin Lukacs, "Neoliberalism Has Conned Us into Fighting Climate Change as Individuals," *The Guardian,* July 17, theguardian.com/environment/true-north/2017/jul/17/neoliberalism-has-conned-us-into-fighting-climate-change-as-individuals and Raj Patel and Jason W. Moore, *A History of the World in Seven Cheap Things: A Guide to Capitalism, Nature, and the Future of the Planet* (Oakland: University of California Press, 2017), 204–205 for discussion of this in environmental contexts.

12 Mary Louise Fellows and Sherene Razack, "The Race to Innocence: Confronting Hierarchical Relations among Women," *Journal of Gender, Race, and Justice* 1 (1998): 335-352; Eve Tuck and K. Wayne Yang, "Decolonization Is Not a Metaphor," *Decolonization: Indigeneity, Education and Society* 1, 1 (2012): 1–40.

13 It was this shared interest in wrestling with ideas, with theory, in movement-grounded rather than scholarly ways that attracted me to *Upping the Anti: A Journal of Theory and Action* (uppingtheanti.org). I have never been part of the editorial collective — the crew whose huge amounts of unpaid labour make each issue possible — but I have been on its advisory board for more than fifteen years. I greatly appreciate the contribution the journal makes in terms of movement-relevant ideas and I am very glad I have had the opportunity to learn from it.

chapter one

1 This section provides only the most basic introduction to hearing. As it makes clear, this book is not about hearing but about listening, and listening as understood in a deliberately multi-sensory way. But if you want to learn more about hearing, there are many resources out there, for instance, Wayne Olsen, *Mayo Clinic on Hearing* (Rochester: Mayo Clinic, 2003) and Christopher J. Plack, *The Sense of Hearing, 3rd Edition* (Milton Park: Taylor & Francis, 2018).

2 Jonathan Sterne, *The Audible Past: Cultural Origins of Sound Reproduction* (Durham: Duke University Press, 2003), 15.

3 Sterne, *The Audible Past*, 5.

4 Sterne, *The Audible Past*, 15.

5 Sterne, *The Audible Past*, 18.

6 For instance, H-Dirksen L. Bauman (ed.), *Open Your Eyes: Deaf Studies Talking* (Minneapolis: University of Minnesota Press, 2008).

7 Various aspects of this phenomenon are subject to ongoing neurobiological investigation. See, for instance, Bethany Brookshire, "How Brains Filter the Signal from the Noise," *Science News*, April 29, 2014, sciencenews.org/blog/scicurious/how-brains-filter-signal-noise; Brenda Kelley Kim, "Say What? How the Brain Filters Out Noise," *labroots*, December 26, 2016, labroots.com/trending/neuroscience/4877/what-brain-filters-noise; *NYU Langone Health*, "A Scientist Maps the Brain's Sensory Switchboard & Opens New Channels to Treat Mental Disorders," 2015, nyulangone.org/news/node/2213; and *Neuroscience News.com*, "How Our Brain Filters Sounds," September 6, 2019, neurosciencenews.com/sound-filter-14882/.

8 Paulo Freire, *Pedagogy of the Oppressed: 30th Anniversary Edition* (New York: Continuum, 2000), 76.

9 Freire, *Pedagogy of the Oppressed*, 72.

10 See, for instance, Debra L. Worthington and Margaret E. Fitch-Hauser, *Listening: Processes, Functioning, and Competency, Second Edition* (New York: Routledge, 2018), 8–17, for a brief overview of some of these models, grounded in current scholarly research on listening. This section draws on that passage and on the book more broadly.
11 Worthington and Fitch-Hauser, *Listening*, 25–40.
12 For a fascinating look at the biological infrastructure that different species have for taking up sensory inputs and what that means for how they sense the world, see Ed Yong, *An Immense World: How Animal Senses Reveal the Hidden Realms Around Us* (Toronto: Alfred A. Knopf Canada, 2022).
13 I first encountered this distinction between propositional and non-propositional knowledge in a conversation with Alexis Shotwell many years ago. Thanks, Alexis!
14 Sterne, *The Audible Past*.
15 See, for instance, Himani Bannerji, *The Dark Side of the Nation: Essays on Multiculturalism, Nationalism, and Gender* (Toronto: Canadian Scholars' Press, 2000); Eva Mackey, *The House of Difference: Cultural Politics and National Identity in Canada* (Toronto: University of Toronto Press, 2002); and Sunera Thobani, *Exalted Subjects: Studies in the Making of Race and Nation in Canada* (Toronto: University of Toronto Press, 2007).
16 Antonio Gramsci, *Selections from the Prison Notebooks of Antonio Gramsci* (London: Lawrence & Wishart, 1976).
17 David Graeber and David Wengrow, *The Dawn of Everything: A New History of Humanity* (Toronto: Signal, 2021), 97.
18 See, for instance, Aimee Carillo Rowe, *Power Lines: On the Subject of Feminist Alliances* (Durham: Duke University Press, 2008) and its examination of how transracial feminist alliances form (or not) in academic contexts. It does not centre listening, but it still illustrates the ways in which affective investments at the interpersonal level can lead to being in new relational contexts, which can then transform political commitments, and hence fundamental ways of taking in, taking up, and making meaning from the world.
19 Nancy C.M. Hartsock, *Money, Sex, and Power: Toward a Feminist Historical Materialism* (Boston: Northeastern University Press, 1985); Sandra Harding, *The Science Question in Feminism* (Ithaca: Cornell University Press, 1986); Patricia Hill Collins, *Black Feminist Thought: Knowledge, Consciousness, and the Politics of Empowerment* (New York: Routledge, 2009); Dorothy E. Smith, *Institutional Ethnography: A Sociology for People* (Lanham: Altamira, 2005); Charles W. Mills, *The Racial Contract* (Ithaca: Cornell University Press, 1999); Shannon Sullivan and Nancy Tuana, *Race and Epistemologies of Ignorance* (Albany: State University of New York Press, 2007). Note that Smith's approach to standpoint is different from the others — see Chapter 3 for more about her work, including her use of standpoint.
20 Hill Collins, *Black Feminist Thought*; Kimberlé Crenshaw, "Mapping the Margins: Intersectionality, Identity Politics, and Violence against Women of Color," *Stanford Law Review* 43, 6 (1991), 1241; Keeanga-Yamahtta Taylor, *How We Get Free: Black Feminism and the Combahee River Collective* (Chicago: Haymarket Books, 2017); Audre Lorde, *Sister Outsider: Essays and Speeches* (Trumansberg: Crossing Press, 1984); Himani Bannerji, *Thinking Through: Essays on Feminism, Marxism and Anti-Racism* (Toronto: Women's Press, 1995).

chapter two

1. For most of the people reading this book, I am guessing that this is probably more or less true, and I am letting that guide how I frame things. But it is important to acknowledge that what I am saying could be taken up more expansively. For one thing, this orientation towards listening is probably culturally specific. Certainly, what we count as a voice, as communicative, even as a person depends a lot on how we understand the world and no doubt shapes the bounds and focus of our listening. As I understand it, many Indigenous worldviews conceptualize sentience, agency, and communication more broadly than currently dominant Western notions allow. Though they are marginalized today, there are long histories of similar ideas in the West as well (Amitav Ghosh, *The Nutmeg's Curse: Parables for a Planet in Crisis* [Chicago: University of Chicago Press, 2021], 37–39). There are also theorists from a wide range of backgrounds who are working today in Western scholarly traditions who are trying to push us to think in new ways about things like communication and agency, extending them far beyond how we might usually define them (e.g., Karen Barad, *Meeting the Universe Halfway: Quantum Physics and the Entanglement of Matter and Meaning* (Durham: Duke University Press, 2007); Donna J. Haraway, *When Species Meet* (Minneapolis: University of Minnesota Press, 2007)). I see great value in these understandings, but I do not take them up here.
2. Douglas Stone and Sheila Heen, *Thanks for the Feedback: The Science and Art of Receiving Feedback Well (Even When it is Offbase, Unfair, Poorly Delivereed, and, Frankly, You're Not in the Mood)* (New York: Viking, 2014), 234.
3. Max H. Bazerman, *The Power of Noticing: What the Best Leaders See* (New York: Simon & Schuster, 2014); Frances Cole Jones, *How to Wow: Proven Strategies for Presenting Your Ideas, Persuading Your Audience, and Perfecting Your Image* (New York: Ballantine Books, 2008); Ron Taffel, *Childhood Unbound: Saving Our Kids' Best Selves — Confident Parenting in a World of Change* (New York: Free Press, 2009); Jim Gray, *How Leaders Speak: Essential Rules for Engaging and Inspiring Others* (Toronto: Dundurn Press, 2010); Anthony E. Wolf, *I'd Listen to My Parents If They'd Just Shut Up: What to Say and Not Say When Parenting Teens* (New York: Harper, 2011); Sheri Van Dijk, *Relationship Skills 101 for Teens: Your Guide to Dealing with Daily Drama, Stress, and Difficult Emotions Using DBT* (Oakland: Instant Help Books, 2015); Sakyong Mipham, *The Lost Art of Good Conversation: A Mindful Way to Connect with Others and Enrich Everyday Life* (New York: Harmony Books, 2017); Meg-John Barker and Justin Hancock, *Enjoy Sex (How, When and If You Want To): A Practical and Inclusive Guide* (London: Icon Books, 2017). It doesn't take much effort to find many, many, many other relevant titles.
4. Gray, *How Leaders Speak*.
5. Wolf, *I'd Listen to My Parents*, 75.
6. Loni Coombs, "Six Tips for Effective Listening," *Dr. Phil*, 2013, drphil.com/advice/six-tips-for-effective-listening/.
7. Phil McGraw, "Dr. Phil's 6 Rules of Talking and Listening," *Oprah.com*, oprah.com/relationships/dr-phils-six-rules-of-talking-and-listening.

8   Leil Lowndes, *How to Talk to Anyone: 92 Little Tricks for Big Success in Relationships* (Columbus: McGraw Hill, 2003), 80, 50, 75, 258.
9   Margaret J. Wheatley, *Turning to One Another: Simple Conversations to Restore Hope to the Future, Expanded 2nd Ed.* (San Francisco: Berrett-Koehler, 2009); Mipham, *The Lost Art of Good Conversation*; Rebecca Z. Shafir, *The Zen of Listening: Mindful Communication in the Age of Distraction* (Wheaten: Quest Books, 2003); Adam S. McHugh, *The Listening Life: Embracing Attentiveness in a World of Distraction* (Downers Grove: IVP Books, 2015); Mark Goulston, *Just Listen: Discover the Secret to Getting Through to Absolutely Anyone* (New York: American Management Association, 2010); Michael P. Nichols, *The Lost Art of Listening: How Learning to Listen Can Improve Relationships* (New York: Guilford Press, 2009); Worthington and Fitch-Hauser, *Listening*.
10 Wheatley, *Turning to One Another*.
11 Shafir, *The Zen of Listening*; Mipham, *The Lost Art of Good Conversation*.
12 McHugh, *The Listening Life*.
13 Worthington and Fitch-Hauser, *Listening*.
14 Goulston, *Just Listen*.
15 Nichols, *The Lost Art of Listening*.
16 Richard Seymour, *The Twittering Machine* (London: The Indigo Press, 2019).
17 Leanne Betasamosake Simpson, *As We Have Always Done: Indigenous Freedom Through Radical Resistance* (Minneapolis: University of Minnesota Press, 2017), 8.
18 Pamela Palmater, *Indigenous Nationhood: Empowering Grassroots Citizens* (Halifax and Winnipeg: Fernwood Publishing, 2015), 1.
19 Takudzwa Hillary Chiwanza, "'Hide Nothing from the Masses ... Tell No Lies ... Claim No Easy Victories' — Extracts From Amilcar Cabral's 1965 Party Directive," *Zimsphere*, July 10, 2023, zimsphere.co.zw/2023/07/hide-nothing-from-the-masses-tell-no-lies-amilcar-cabral.html?m=1.
20 Harsha Walia, "Moving Beyond a Politics of Solidarity Towards a Practice of Decolonization," in *Organize! Building from the Local for Global Justice*, eds. Aziz Choudry, Jill Hanley, and Eric Shragge (Oakland: PM Press; Toronto: Between the Lines, 2012), 251–252.
21 Judy Rebick, *Ten Thousand Roses: The Making of a Feminist Revolution* (Toronto: Penguin Canada, 2005), xi.
22 Norman Nawrocki, "Listen to the Music: Work the Music, Organize the Community," in *Organize! Building from the Local for Global Justice*, eds. Aziz Choudry, Jill Hanley, and Eric Shragge (Oakland: PM Press; Toronto: Between the Lines, 2012).
23 Saul D. Alinsky, *Rules for Radicals: A Pragmatic Primer for Realistic Radicals* (New York: Vintage Books, 1989), 68–69, 81.
24 Kelly Hayes and Mariame Kaba, *Let This Radicalize You: Organizing and the Revolution of Reciprocal Care* (Chicago: Haymarket Books, 2023), 188, see also 187–192. See also Mariame Kaba, *We Do This 'Til We Free Us: Abolitionist Organizing and Transforming Justice* (Chicago: Haymarket Books, 2021).
25 Michael Novick, "Lessons from a Lifetime of Antiracist and Antifascist Struggle: A Memoir and Analysis" in *¡No Pasarán!: Antifascist Dispatches from a World in Crisis*, ed. Shane Burley (Chico: AK Press, 2022), 137.

26 Leah Hunt-Hendrix and Astra Taylor, *Solidarity: The Past, Present, and Future of a World-Changing Idea* (New York: Pantheon Books, 2024), 294.
27 Mark Nowak, "The Essentials of Socialist Writing," *Jacobin*, December 16, 2016, jacobinmag.com/2016/12/socialist-writing-publishing-books-reading/.
28 adrienne maree brown, *Emergent Strategy: Shaping Change, Changing Worlds* (Chico: AK Press, 2017), 5.
29 Nichols, *The Lost Art of Listening*, 62.

chapter three

1 Thu-Huong Ha, "John Donne's Solemn 400-Year-Old Poem Against Isolationism Is Resonating Today," *Quartz*, June 24, 2016, qz.com/716088/john-donnes-solemn-400-year-old-poem-against-isolationism-is-resonating-with-brits-today/.
2 Alfred Lord Tennyson, "Ulysses," *All Poetry*, allpoetry.com/poem/8473279-Ulysses-by-Alfred-Lord-Tennyson.
3 Donna Haraway, *A Cyborg Manifesto: Science, Technology, and Socialist-Feminism in the Late Twentieth Century* (New York: Routledge, 1991); Linda Lorraine Nash, *Inescapable Ecologies: A History of Environment, Disease, and Knowledge* (Berkeley: University of California Press, 2007); Alexis Shotwell, *Against Purity: Living Ethically in Compromised Times* (Minneapolis: University of Minnesota Press, 2016), 77–106.
4 David Camfield, *We Can Do Better: Ideas for Changing Society* (Halifax and Winnipeg: Fernwood Publishing, 2017), 1.
5 Camfield, *We Can Do Better*, 2.
6 Georg Lukács, *History and Class Consciousness: Studies in Marxist Dialectics* (Cambridge: MIT Press, 1972).
7 Smith, *Institutional Ethnography*.
8 Caelie Frampton et al. (eds.), *Sociology for Changing the World: Social Movements/Social Research* (Halifax: Fernwood Publishing, 2006), 37.
9 Frampton et al., *Sociology for Changing*, 37.
10 Karl Marx and Frederick Engels, *Manifesto of the Communist Party*, trans. Samuel Moore and Frederick Engels (Marxist Internet Archive: 2004), 16, marxists.org/archive/marx/works/download/pdf/Manifesto.pdf.
11 Richard Seymour, *The Liberal Defence of Murder* (London: Verso, 2012); Domenico Losurdo, *Liberalism: A Counter-History*, trans. Gregory Elliott (London: Verso, 2014); Pankaj Mishra, *Age of Anger: A History of the Present* (New York: Farrar, Straus and Giroux, 2017).
12 C.B. MacPherson, *The Political Theory of Possessive Individualism: Hobbes to Locke* (Don Mills: Oxford University Press Canada, 2011).
13 Helena Rosenblatt, *The Lost History of Liberalism: From Ancient Rome to the Twenty-First Century* (Princeton: Princeton University Press, 2018).
14 See David Harvey, *A Brief History of Neoliberalism* (New York: Oxford University Press, 2007), for a widely read account of neoliberalism. To get a sense of the ways in which it was a response to the struggles of colonized peoples and of its impacts on formerly colonized peoples, see Vijay Prashad, *The Darker Nations: A People's History of the Third World* (New York: New Press, 2008) and Vijay Prashad, *The Poorer Nations: A Possible History of the Global South* (London: Verso, 2012).

For an account that understands the changes of the neoliberal era as a response to struggle from below and that explores some of the new forms that struggle took during its early stages, see Michael Hardt, *The Subversive Seventies* (New York: Oxford University Press, 2023). For a brief overview that focuses on Canada and has pointers to lots of other sources, see Scott Neigh, *Resisting the State*, 159–187.

15   Mishra, *Age of Anger*, 12.
16   Billy-Ray Belcourt, *A History of My Brief Body* (Toronto: Hamish Hamilton, 2020), 127.
17   See Chapter 8 for a more detailed discussion of the importance of knowledge produced during collective struggle.
18   Michele Dillon, *Introduction to Sociological Theory: Theorists, Concepts, and Their Applicability to the Twenty-First Century, Second Edition* (Chichester: John Wiley & Sons, 2014).
19   One scholarly approach to practices that enact this kind of attention is discourse analysis. See, for example, Teun A. van Dijk, *Discourse Studies: A Multidisciplinary Introduction, Second Edition* (Los Angeles: SAGE Publications, 2011); Norman Fairclough, *Discourse and Social Change* (Cambridge: Polity Press, 1993); and Norman Fairclough, *Critical Discourse Analysis: The Critical Study of Language, Second Edition* (New York: Routledge, 2013).
20   For instance, Patricia Hill Collins notes, "the more legitimate intersectional scholarship becomes in colleges and universities, the more abstract and disengaged it can become from actual social relations" (*On Intellectual Activism* [Philadelphia: Temple University Press, 2013], 234), and elsewhere writes (though not explicitly linking it to intersectionality), "A more recent pattern of suppression involves incorporating, changing, and thereby depoliticizing Black feminist ideas" (*Black Feminist Thought*, 8). Professor of African American studies Keeanga-Yamahtta Taylor observes with reference to Black feminist ideas that "political analysis outside of political movements and struggles becomes abstract, discourse driven, and disconnected from the radicalism that made it powerful in the first place" and published an entire book whose purpose she identified as "an effort to reconnect the radical roots of Black feminist analysis and practice to contemporary organizing" (*How We Get Free*, 13).
21   Crenshaw, "Mapping the Margins."
22   Audre Lorde, "Learning from the 60s," *Black Past*, August 12, 2012. blackpast.org/african-american-history/1982-audre-lorde-learning-60s/
23   Taylor, *How We Get Free*, 15.
24   Hill Collins, *Black Feminist Thought*, 246.
25   Smith passed away at the age of 96 while I was working on getting this chapter from first draft to second draft. I did not know her and only had the opportunity to meet her once, but I have learned a lot from her work and from the work of people who learned from her (particularly including, as I mentioned in the Acknowledgements, Gary Kinsman). See Himani Bannerji, "Remembering Dorothy Smith (1926–2022)," *Upping the Anti* 23 (2022): 46 and William K. Carroll, "Remembering Dorothy E. Smith: A Socialist Studies Tribute," *Socialist Studies/Etudes socialistes* 16, 1 (2022). For much more detail than I provide about the theoretical basis and practical methods of institutional ethnography, see especially Smith, *Institutional Ethnography*, also Dorothy Smith, *The Conceptual*

Practices of Power: A Feminist Sociology of Knowledge (Boston: Northeastern University Press, 1990); Dorothy E. Smith, *Writing the Social: Critique, Theory and Investigations* (Toronto: University of Toronto Press, 1999); Marie Campbell and Frances Gregor, *Mapping Social Relations: A Primer in Doing Institutional Ethnography* (Aurora: Garamond Press, 2002); Frampton et al., *Sociology for Changing the World*; and really anything by Dorothy Smith that you can get your hands on.

26 Smith, *Institutional Ethnography*, 31.
27 Smith, *Institutional Ethnography*, 28.
28 Smith, *Institutional Ethnography*, 12.
29 Smith, *Institutional Ethnography*, 25. Though her approach to sociology is not the same as Smith's, Patricia Hill Collins also noted, "Much of my formal academic training has been designed to show me that I must alienate myself from my communities, my family, and even my own self in order to produce credible intellectual work. Instead of viewing the everyday as a negative influence on my theorizing, I tried to see how the everyday actions and ideas of the Black women in my life reflected the theoretical issues I claimed were so important to them" (*Black Feminist Thought*, ix).
30 George W. Smith, "Political Activist as Ethnographer," in *Sociology for Changing the World: Social Movements/Social Research*, eds. Caelie Frampton et al. (Halifax: Fernwood Publishing, 2006), 48. (Note that George Smith was unrelated to but a student of Dorothy Smith. We encounter his work in more detail in Chapter 8.)

chapter four

1 Unlike most of the book both before and after, in this chapter I more consistently enter listening through my own experience of it. As someone currently without significant sensory impairments, a big part of my own listening is auditory. For that reason, in circumstances where it leads to less cumbersome phrasing, I use the language of "hearing" more freely here than in the rest of the book.
2 Holloway, *Change the World Without Taking Power*, 1. I would be inclined to keep the naming of the social totality that induces us to scream more open, more unstable, more explicit in its recognition of the interconnection mentioned in the last chapter, but capitalism, particularly when understood expansively, is certainly one crucial way of naming it.
3 Holloway, *Change the World*, 7.
4 Holloway, *Change the World*, 8.
5 The insight that what we hear first and foremost when we hear the voice is another unique, embodied self comes from Adriana Cavarero, *For More Than One Voice: Toward a Philosophy of Vocal Expression,* trans. Paul A. Kottman (Stanford: Stanford University Press, 2005), though I do not follow the same deeply philosophical path that she takes from that insight.
6 John Holloway and Marina Sitrin, "Against and Beyond the State: An Interview with John Holloway," *Upping the Anti* 4 (2007): 58.
7 Two important sources that helped me clarify how I wanted to talk about this aspect of listening were Dylan Robinson, *Hungry Listening: Resonant Theory for Indigenous Sound Studies* (Minneapolis: University of Minnesota Press, 2020),

58–62 and J. Martin Daughtry, "Acoustic Palimpsests and the Politics of Listening," *Music and Politics* 7, 1 (Winter 2013), 1–34, which talk about listening using the metaphor of the palimpsest. I draw on the idea of layering in a direct way here, but I opted not to use the figure of the palimpsest. Still, I find both the imagery and the discussion in those two sources to be useful for thinking richly about listening that digs deeply into a moment and extends beyond it.
8   Again, this formulation borrows from Cavarero, *For More Than One*, though does not necessarily use it in the same way.
9   Christina Sharpe, *Ordinary Notes* (Toronto: Alfred A. Knopf Canada, 2023), 277.

chapter five

1   If by some rare chance you read this and remember: I'm so sorry, Allison!
2   As Christina Sharpe puts it, "The architectures of violence fracture we; affect does not reach us in the same ways" (*Ordinary Notes*, 33).
3   Mills, *The Racial Contract*.
4   For a stark articulation of this idea by the great James Baldwin, see his *James Baldwin: The Last Interview and Other Conversations* (Brooklyn: Melville House, 2014), 6–7.
5   Crystal M. Fleming, *How to Be Less Stupid about Race: On Racism, White Supremacy, and the Racial Divide* (Boston: Beacon Press, 2018), 2.
6   Fleming, *How to Be Less*, 27.
7   bell hooks, *Feminism Is for Everybody: Passionate Politics* (New York: Routledge, 2015), 21.
8   Shane Burley, "'Kops and Klan Go Hand in Hand': An Interview with Kelly Hayes," in *¡No Pasarán! Antifascist Dispatches from a World in Crisis*, ed. Shane Burley (Chico: AK Press, 2022), 380.
9   Fleming, *How to Be Less*, 37, emphasis in original.
10 Robin Maynard, *Policing Black Lives: State Violence in Canada from Slavery to the Present* (Halifax and Winnipeg: Fernwood Publishing, 2017).
11 Whether this heightened scrutiny is part of being targeted for harm depends on who you are and what the context is. In my experience, there may be a rush of self-consciousness at being an out-of-place cisgender white man in a space that is predominantly racialized and/or women, but nothing like the same potentially oppressive dynamics as occur when the situation is reversed.
12 There are also some specific scenarios where a tendency towards particular kinds of failures of listening might develop in the course of trying to survive oppression — it is complex and sometimes can be messy, and it isn't just a simple binary.
13 Ijeoma Oluo, *So You Want to Talk about Race* (New York: Seal Press, 2019), 162–78.
14 Clive Stafford Smith, "Welcome to 'The Disco,'" *Guardian*, June 19, 2008, theguardian.com/world/2008/jun/19/usa.guantanamo.
15 e.g. Lowndes, *How to Talk*; Goulston, *Just Listen*.
16 Donald Rumsfeld, *Rumsfeld's Rules: Leadership Lessons in Business, Politics, War, and Life* (New York: HarperCollins Publishers, 2013), 326.
17 Goulston, *Just Listen*, 170.
18 Roxanne Dunbar-Ortiz, *An Indigenous Peoples' History of the United States* (Boston: Beacon Press, 2014), 199–200.

19 Shafir, *The Zen of Listening*, 12.
20 Bob Moser, "The Soul-Crushing Legacy of Billy Graham," *Rolling Stone*, February 23, 2018, rollingstone.com/politics/politics-news/the-soul-crushing-legacy-of-billy-graham-200536/.
21 Shafir, *The Zen of Listening*, 54.
22 The many examples include Josh Eidelson, "Whose Walmart?: Workers Crash Walmart's Party," *The Nation*, June 17, 2013, thenation.com/article/archive/whose-walmart-workers-crash-walmarts-party/; Rachel Quednau, "The Other Problem with Walmart," *Strong Towns*, February 25, 2015, strongtowns.org/journal/2015/2/23/the-other-problem-with-walmart; Meghan Hall, "Walmart Slammed as 'Unsafe and Reckless' Employer in 'Dirty Dozen' Report," *Sourcing Journal*, April 25, 2024, sourcingjournal.com/topics/labor/walmart-national-council-for-occupational-safety-and-health-cosh-workers-rights-gun-violence-506864/; Austin Frerick, *Barons: Money, Power, and the Corruption of America's Food Industry* (Washington: Island Press, 2024); Hugo Meunier, *Walmart: Diary of an Associate* (Halifax: Fernwood, 2019).
23 Stephanie Russell-Kraft, "The Survivor Who Broke the Shambhala Sexual Assault Story," *Columbia Journalism Review*, May 7, 2019, cjr.org/the_profile/shambhala-buddhist-project-sunshine.php; Michelle Boorstein, "Famed Buddhist Nun Pema Chodron Retires, Cites Handling of Sexual Misconduct Allegations Against Her Group's Leader," *Washington Post*, January 17, 2020, washingtonpost.com/religion/2020/01/17/famed-buddhist-nun-pema-chodron-retires-cites-handling-sexual-misconduct-charges-against-group-leader/; Nina Müller, "Canadian Yoga Teacher Accuses Shambhala of Seeking to Evict Him for Speaking Out Against Its Leader," *Buddhistdoor Global*, August 24, 2021, buddhistdoor.net/news/canadian-yoga-teacher-accuses-shambhala-of-seeking-to-evict-him-for-speaking-out-against-its-leader/.
24 Edward Said, *Orientalism, 25th Anniversary Edition* (New York: Vintage Books, 1994).
25 Linda Tuhiwai Smith, *Decolonizing Methodologies: Research and Indigenous Peoples* (London and New York: Zed Books and Dunedin: University of Otago Press, 1999).
26 Smith, *Decolonizing Methodologies*, 2.
27 Smith, *Decolonizing Methodologies*, 24.
28 Smith, *Decolonizing Methodologies*, 39.
29 Smith, *Decolonizing Methodologies*, 25.
30 Robyn Maynard and Leanne Betasamosake Simpson, *Rehearsals for Living* (Toronto: Alfred A. Knopf Canada, 2022), 20, emphasis in original.
31 Maynard and Simpson, *Rehearsals for Living*, 23.
32 Katherine McKittrick (ed.), *Sylvia Wynter: On Being Human as Praxis* (Durham and London: Duke University Press, 2015).
33 Katherine McKittrick, "Yours in the Intellectual Struggle," in *Sylvia Wynter: On Being Human as Praxis*, ed. Katherine McKittrick (Durham and London: Duke University Press, 2015), 3.
34 McKittrick, "Yours in the Intellectual Struggle," 7.
35 Sylvia Wynter and Katherine McKittrick, "Unparalleled Catastrophe for Our Species? Or, to Give Humanness a Different Future: Conversations" in *Syvlia

Wynter: On Being Human as Praxis, ed. Katherine McKittrick (Durham and London: Duke University Press, 2015), 10.
36 Édouard Glissant, *Poetics of Relation*, trans. Betsy Wing (Ann Arbor: University of Michigan Press, 1997).
37 Robinson, *Hungry Listening*.
38 bell hooks, *Black Looks: Race and Representation* (Boston: South End Press, 1992), 21–39.
39 See, for instance, John Clarke, "The War on the Poor in the Age of Austerity," *Canadian Dimension*, February 4, 2020, canadiandimension.com/articles/view/the-war-on-the-poor-in-the-age-of-austerity for a brief overview of social assistance and its role, and Neigh, *Resisting the State*, 159–187 for some relevant history and references.

chapter six

1 An important early catalyst for me to think about complicity and what it means was the work of Sherene Razack, including *Looking White People in the Eye: Gender, Race, and Culture in Courtrooms and Classrooms* (Toronto: University of Toronto Press, 1998).
2 "Everyday living" used in this way is my own formulation. "Everyday compliance" and "everyday resistance" are from James C. Scott, *Weapons of the Weak: Everyday Forms of Peasant Resistance* (New Haven and London: Yale University Press, 1985) — for instance, see his use of "everyday compliance" at p. 289 of that book.
3 Scott, *Weapons of the Weak*, 289.
4 This of course places it in a particular field of professionalized listening and knowledge production tightly bound up in the last five centuries of imperial/colonial relations, which we touched on in a limited way in Chapter 5. While still being open to critique of Scott's work along those lines, I am obviously choosing to listen and learn from it specifically with regards to the concept of everyday resistance.
5 Scott, *Weapons of the Weak*, 350.
6 W.E.B. Du Bois, *Black Reconstruction in America 1860–1880* (New York: The Free Press, 1999).
7 Anton Pannekoek, *Workers' Councils* (Oakland: AK Press, 2003), 8.
8 Grace C. Lee, Pierre Chaulieu, and J.R. Johnson, *Facing Reality* (Detroit: Correspondence Publishing Company, 1958), 5.
9 Frances Fox Piven and Richard A. Cloward, *Poor People's Movements: Why They Succeed, How They Fail* (New York: Vintage Books, 1979).
10 Scott, *Weapons of the Weak*, xvi.
11 Scott, *Weapons of the Weak*, xvi.
12 Scott, *Weapons of the Weak*, xvi.
13 Robin D.G. Kelley, *Race Rebels: Culture, Politics, and the Black Working Class* (New York: The Free Press, 1996), 35–53.
14 Kelley, *Race Rebels*, 48.
15 Kelley, *Race Rebels*, 45.
16 Kelley, *Race Rebels*, 51.
17 Kelley, *Race Rebels*, 55-75.

18 Kelley, *Race Rebels*, 61.
19 Kelley, *Race Rebels*, 75.
20 Kelley, *Race Rebels*, 1–4.
21 Kelley, *Race Rebels*, 1.
22 Hill Collins, *Black Feminist Thought*.
23 Hill Collins, *Black Feminist Thought*, 76-106.
24 Hill Collins, *Black Feminist Thought*, 57, 112.
25 Hill Collins, *Black Feminist Thought*, 217.
26 Hill Collins, *Black Feminist Thought*, 129.
27 Hill Collins, *Black Feminist Thought*, 217.
28 Jennifer Lynn Stoever, *The Sonic Color Line: Race and the Cultural Politics of Listening* (New York: New York University Press, 2016), 69.
29 Stoever, *The Sonic Color Line*, 83.
30 Asef Bayat, *Life as Politics: How Ordinary People Change the Middle East, Second Edition* (Stanford: Stanford University Press, 2013).
31 Bayat, *Life as Politics*, 18.
32 Bayat, *Life as Politics*, 21.
33 Many other sources are no doubt crucial to developing a deep understanding of these questions, but some that have helped me include Incite! Women of Color Against Violence, *Color of Violence: The Incite! Anthology* (Cambridge: South End Press, 2006); Ching-In Chen, Jai Dulani, and Leah Lakshmi Piepzna-Samarasinha (eds.), *The Revolution Starts at Home: Confronting Intimate Partner Violence within Activist Communities* (Brooklyn and Boston: South End Press, 2011); Leah Lakshmi Piepzna-Samarasinha, *Care Work: Dreaming Disability Justice* (Vancouver: Arsenal Pulp Press, 2018); Kaba, *We Do This 'Til*; and Ardath Whynacht, *Insurgent Love: Abolition and Domestic Homicide* (Halifax and Winnipeg: Fernwood Publishing, 2021). See also Scott Neigh, "Transformative Justice as Response to Sexual and Gendered Violence," *Talking Radical Radio* (podcast), May 14, 2019, talkingradical.ca/2019/05/14/trr-third_eye_collective/ and "Prison Abolition and How We Respond to the Worst Forms of Gendered Violence," *Talking Radical Radio* (podcast), October 12, 2021, talkingradical.ca/2021/10/12/radio-prison-abolition-and-how-we-respond-to-the-worst-forms-of-gendered-violence/.
34 Simpson, *As We Have Always Done*.
35 Simpson, *As We Have Always Done*, 17.
36 Simpson, *As We Have Always Done*, 22; Glen Sean Coulthard, *Red Skin, White Masks: Rejecting the Colonial Politics of Recognition* (Minneapolis: University of Minnesota Press, 2014).
37 Simpson, *As We Have Always Done*, 21.
38 Simpson, *As We Have Always Done*, 17.
39 Kelley, *Race Rebels*, 230.
40 I appreciate why he does that and respect his definitions, but in the context I am writing about here, what he describes fits with how I am using the term "everyday resistance."
41 Kelley, *Race Rebels*, 230.

chapter seven

1 There is, obviously, a bit of a tension in how I'm talking about this. Anything that you do becomes part of your everyday life, whatever it happens to be. So, for instance, if you go to a demonstration, that becomes part of your everyday life, and does not somehow enter some separate, non-everyday sphere. The distinction I am making is between everyday resistance as discussed in Chapter 6 and forms of resistance that go beyond that.

2 Francesca Polletta, *Freedom Is an Endless Meeting: Democracy in American Social Movements* (Chicago: University of Chicago Press, 2004).

3 See, for instance, Anne Crocker, "Consciousness Raising — What It Is and What It Isn't," in *Canadian Women's Issues, Volume 1: Strong Voices*, eds. Ruth Roach Pierson et al. (Toronto: James Lorimer and Company, 1993), 37–9 and Sara Evans, *Personal Politics: The Roots of Women's Liberation in the Civil Rights Movement and the New Left* (New York: Vintage Books, 1980) to read about classic feminist consciousness raising groups on this model. But organic instances of similar, if usually not clearly identified, processes where conversation about shared experiences are important elements of moving towards collective action happen all the time — see Scott Neigh's *Talking Radical Radio* podcasts: "A Solidarity Fund by and for Trans Women," March 26, 2019, talkingradical.ca/2019/03/26/trr-taking_what_we_need/; "Long COVID: Growing Advocacy for Recognition, Research, and Rehab," April 27, 2021, talkingradical.ca/2021/04/27/radio-long-covid-growing-advocacy-for-recognition-research-and-rehab/; and "Mobilizing Class-Privileged Youth to Work for Social Justice," June 8, 2021, talkingradical.ca/2021/06/08/radio-mobilizing-class-privileged-youth-to-work-for-social-justice/, among many others.

4 Scott Neigh, "A Rare Space for Social Movements to Reflect and Theorize," *Talking Radical Radio* (podcast), May 11, 2021, talkingradical.ca/2021/05/11/radio-a-rare-space-for-social-movements-to-reflect-and-theorize/.

5 Scott Neigh, "Indigenous Women Rising in the Face of Violence and Injustice," *Talking Radical Radio* (podcast), April 23, 2019, talkingradical.ca/2019/04/23/trr-red_women_rising/; and "Trans Youth Challenging Barriers to Gender-Affirming Health Care," *Talking Radical Radio* (podcast), June 25, 2019, talkingradical.ca/2019/06/25/trr-saefty_ottawa/.

6 Scott Neigh, "Building the Skills of Social Movement Organizers," *Talking Radical Radio* (podcast), April 9, 2019, talkingradical.ca/2019/04/09/trr-organize_bc/; and "Social Movements and Radical Legal Support Organizing," *Talking Radical Radio* (podcast), April 20, 2021, talkingradical.ca/2021/04/20/radio-social-movements-and-radical-legal-support-organizing/.

7 Scott Neigh, "Activist Seniors Raising a Ruckus in Edmonton," *Talking Radical Radio* (podcast), July 30, 2014, talkingradical.ca/2014/07/30/trr-salt_edmonton/; Dana Hatherly, "Indigenous Youth Vacate Minister's Office, Ending 11-Day Occupation for Wet'suwet'en, *CBC*, February 17, 2020, cbc.ca/news/canada/manitoba/coastal-gaslink-opponents-end-occupation-winnipeg-1.5466142.

8 Scott Neigh, "Grassroots Dene People Defending the Land in Northern Saskatchewan," *Talking Radical Radio* (podcast), March 25, 2015, talkingradical.ca/2015/03/25/trr-northern_dene_trappers/; "Mi'kmaq Water Protectors Blocking

Fossil Fuel Infrastructure in Nova Scotia," *Talking Radical Radio* (podcast), March 20, 2018, talkingradical.ca/2018/03/20/trr-alton_gas_resistance/; "A Land Defence Camp Opposing the Line 3 Tar Sands Pipeline," *Talking Radical Radio* (podcast), January 8, 2019, talkingradical.ca/2019/01/08/trr-spirit_of_the_buffalo/; and "Ongoing Wet'suwet'en Resistance to the CGL Pipeline," *Talking Radical Radio* (podcast*)* October 25, 2022, talkingradical.ca/2022/10/25/radio-ongoing-wetsuweten-resistance-to-the-cgl-pipeline/.

9   Scott Neigh, "Direct Action Against Development in Winnipeg," *Talking Radical Radio* (podcast), November 28, 2017, talkingradical.ca/2017/11/28/trr-rooster_town_blockade/; Griff Ferris, Rivka Micklethwaite, and Callum Lynch, "We Took Direct Action Against the UK's Racist Policies, and a Jury Acquitted Us. Resistance Can Succeed," *Guardian*, June 16, 2023, theguardian.com/commentisfree/2023/jun/16/direct-action-uk-policies-deportations-to-jamaica; Nur Dogan and Alex Cosh, "'Israel Arms Embargo Now': Protesters Launch Coordinated Blockades of Canadian Manufacturers," *The Maple*, February 28, 2024, readthemaple.com/israel-arms-embargo-now-protesters-launch-coordinated-blockades-of-canadian-manufacturers/; Janaya Khan, "Organizing Direct Action in the Digital Age," in *Until We Are Free: Reflections on Black Lives Matter in Canada*, eds. Rodney Diverlus, Sandy Hudson, and Syrus Marcus Ware (Regina: University of Regina Press, 2020), 127–29.

10 Azeezah Kanji and AJ Withers, "Encampment Evictions: Another Face of Colonial Violence in Canada," *Al Jazeera*, July 20, 2021. aljazeera.com/opinions/2021/7/20/encampment-evictions-another-face-of-colonial-violence-in-canada; Scott Neigh, "Supporting Homeless Encampments in Halifax," *Talking Radical Radio* (podcast), November 2, 2021. talkingradical.ca/2021/11/02/radio-supporting-homeless-encampments-in-halifax/.

11 Scott Neigh, "Grassroots Revitalization of Indigenous Languages and Traditional Knowledge," *Talking Radical Radio* (podcast), September 16, 2015, talkingradical.ca/2015/09/16/trr_onaman_collective/; and "Revitalizing Indigenous Languages and Cultures," *Talking Radical Radio* (podcast), September 3, 2019, talkingradical.ca/2019/09/03/trr-tiffany_joseph/

12 Simpson, *As We Have Always*, 11–25.

13 This paragraph is inspired by and in the spirit of S.K. Hussan, "You Can't Change the World Alone, but All of Us Can Together," *Medium* (blog), September 18, 2016. medium.com/@hussansk/you-cant-change-the-world-alone-but-all-of-us-can-together-473fb43001ba#.cjqb37tkt, a short blog post by a migrant justice organizer from Toronto (and past *Talking Radical Radio* guest: Scott Neigh, "Individual Injustice, Collective Struggle: Examples from Migrant Justice Organizing," *Talking Radical Radio* (podcast), May 7, 2014, talkingradical.ca/2014/05/07/trr-migrant_justice_collective/). Despite its brevity and simplicity, it really made an impression on me, and I found it particularly powerful and relevant a few months after it was published, when Donald Trump was first elected President of the United States. Whatever else each of us needs to be doing to change the world, in this neoliberal age we need to recognize that one of the most powerful things we can do is start doing things *with others*.

14 Harsha Walia, *Undoing Border Imperialism* (Oakland: AK Press, 2013), 3, emphasis in original.

15 The thinking in this paragraph is inspired by the interview with long-time African Nova Scotian activist Lynn Jones that is the basis of Neigh, *Resisting the State*, 105–27, though the specifics are my own and if I have gotten it wrong, blame me and not Lynn!

16 See, for instance, Chris Dixon, *Another Politics: Talking across Today's Transformative Movements* (Oakland: University of California Press, 2014), 159–62 for a brief discussion of how the binary of activism versus organizing can be useful but can also be used "to broadly dismiss certain kinds of political work and glorify others" (161). I would go a step further and argue that focusing too much on a term that often carries with it set ideas about what supposedly "real" social change work looks like can get in the way of even noticing work that doesn't fit within those bounds.

17 Yes, I am including even this kind of expenditure of affective energy and its role in processing our experiences as work.

18 Michael Hardt argues that even the infamous urban armed groups of the 1970s deployed their actions to a significant extent with a goal of sparking new understandings and narratives in the broader public (*The Subversive Seventies*, 216–32).

19 The language of circulation of struggle comes from autonomist Marxism. See, for instance, Nick Dyer-Witheford, *Cyber-Marx: Cycles and Circuits of Struggle in High-Technology Capitalism* (Urbana and Chicago: University of Illinois Press, 1999); Harry Cleaver, *Reading Capital Politically* (Leeds: Anti/Theses and Edinburgh: AK Press, 2000); Gary Kinsman, "The Politics of Revolution: Learning from Autonomist Marxism," *Upping the Anti* 1 (2005), 41–50 and "Mapping Social Relations of Struggle: Activism, Ethnography, Social Organization," in *Sociology for Changing the World: Social Movements/Social Research*, Caelie Frampton et al. (eds.) (Halifax: Fernwood Publishing, 2006), 133–56.

20 Carrie Kahn, "Battle Cry: Occupy's Messaging Tactics Catch On," *NPR*, December 6, 2011, npr.org/2011/12/06/142999617/battle-cry-occupys-messaging-tactics-catch-on; Rodney Diverlus, Sandy Hudson, and Syrus Marcus Ware (eds.), *Until We Are Free: Reflections on Black Lives Matter in Canada* (Regina: University of Regina Press, 2020).

21 David Sirota, "There's No Way Around It: Spending on Police in the US Is Out of Control," *Jacobin*, June 8, 2020, jacobin.com/2020/06/defund-police-protests-minneapolis-city-council.

22 George Katsiaficas, *The Global Imagination of 1968: Revolution and Counterrevolution* (Oakland: PM Press, 2018). He famously characterizes the kind of circulation of struggle that happened in 1968 as an "eros effect," building on the work of his mentor Herbert Marcuse. I don't find that language to be helpful, so I have not used it.

23 Katsificas, *The Global Imagination*, 45.

24 For example, see CLR James, "The Revolutionary Answer to the Negro Problem in the United States," *Marxists.org*, December 1948, marxists.org/archive/james-clr/works/1948/revolutionary-answer.htm; Robert L. Allen, *Reluctant Reformers: Racism and Social Reform Movements in the United States* (Washington: Howard University Press, 1974); Evans, *Personal Politics*; Cedric J. Robinson, *Black Movements in America* (New York: Routledge, 1997); Robin D.G. Kelley,

Freedom Dreams: The Black Radical Imagination (Boston: Beacon Press, 2002); Nikhil Pal Singh, *Black Is a Country: Race and the Unfinished Struggle for Democracy* (Cambridge and London: Harvard University Press, 2005); Keeanga-Yamahtta Taylor, *From #BlackLivesMatter to Black Liberation* (Chicago: Haymarket Books, 2016).

25 As Toni Morrison once wrote, "Women's liberation flowered best in the soil prepared by black liberation" (*The Source of Self-Regard* (New York: Vintage International, 2020), 87).

26 For some useful general reflections on solidarity, see, for instance, Hunt-Hendrix and Taylor, *Solidarity* and the special journal issue "On Solidarity," *Boston Review* 3 (2023).

27 David Featherstone, *Solidarity: Hidden Histories and Geographies of Internationalism* (London and New York: Zed Books, 2012).

28 Featherstone, *Solidarity*, 1–4.

29 Featherstone, *Solidarity*, 3.

30 For example, see Scott Neigh, "Parents Fighting the Cuts to Public Education in Ontario," *Talking Radical Radio* (podcast), November 26, 2019, talkingradical.ca/2019/11/26/trr-west_end_parents/; "Defending Public Health Care in Alberta," *Talking Radical Radio* (podcast), December 17, 2019, talkingradical.ca/2019/12/17/trr-friends_of_medicare/; "Fighting Austerity in Manitoba in the Middle of a Pandemic," *Talking Radical Radio* (podcast), June 9, 2020, talkingradical.ca/2020/06/09/radio-fighting-austerity-in-manitoba-in-the-middle-of-a-pandemic/; "Standing Up for Students and Public Education in Alberta," *Talking Radical Radio* (podcast), October 20, 2020, talkingradical.ca/2020/10/20/radio-standing-up-for-students-and-public-education-in-alberta/; and "Resisting an Unprecedented Austerity Attack on the University Sector," *Talking Radical Radio* (podcast), March 30, 2021, talkingradical.ca/2021/03/30/radio-resisting-an-unprecedented-austerity-attack-on-the-university-sector/.

31 For example, see Scott Neigh, "Crisis for Abortion Services and Trans Care in New Brunswick," *Talking Radical Radio* (podcast), October 29, 2019, talkingradical.ca/2019/10/29/trr-save_clinic_554/; "The Growing Movement for Free Public Transit," *Talking Radical Radio* (podcast), August 11, 2020, talkingradical.ca/2020/08/11/radio-the-growing-movement-for-free-public-transit/; "Campaigning for $10-a-Day Public Child Care," *Talking Radical Radio* (podcast), September 1, 2020, talkingradical.ca/2020/09/01/radio-campaigning-for-10-a-day-public-child-care/; "A Campaign to Bring Long-term Care into the Public Health Care System," *Talking Radical Radio* (podcast), August 10, 2021, talkingradical.ca/2021/08/10/radio-a-campaign-to-bring-long-term-care-into-the-public-health-care-system/; and "The Fight for Universal Dental Care in Canada," *Talking Radical Radio* (podcast), November 9, 2021, talkingradical.ca/2021/11/09/radio-the-fight-for-universal-dental-care-in-canada/.

32 Gary Kinsman and Patrizia Gentile, *The Canadian War on Queers: National Security as Sexual Regulation* (Vancouver and Toronto: UBC Press, 2010), 21; Gary Kinsman, "Queer Liberation: The Social Organization of Forgetting and the Resistance of Remembering," *Canadian Dimension*, June 22, 2010, canadiandimension.com/articles/view/queer-liberation-the-social-organization-of-forgetting-and-the-resistance-o.

33   Dixon, *Another Politics*, 55.
34   Andrew Cornell, *Oppose and Propose!* (Oakland and Edinburgh: AK Press, 2011); Dixon, *Another Politics*.
35   Kevin Van Meter, *Guerillas of Desire: Notes on Everyday Resistance and Organizing to Make a Revolution Possible* (Oakland and Edinburgh: AK Press, 2017), 7–8.
36   Incite! (eds.), *The Revolution Will Not Be Funded: Beyond the Non-Profit Industrial Complex* (Durham: Duke University Press, 2017).
37   Shotwell, *Against Purity*.
38   Rinaldo Walcott and Idil Abdillahi, *BlackLife: Post-BLM and the Struggle for Freedom* (Winnipeg: ARP Books, 2019).
39   Walcott and Abdillahi, *BlackLife*, 91.
40   Walcott and Abdillahi, *BlackLife*, 94.
41   Walcott and Abdillahi, *BlackLife*, 91.
42   Maynard and Simpson, *Rehearsals for Living*, 195.
43   Evans, *Personal Politics*.
44   Allen, *Reluctant Reformers*.
45   Priyamvada Gopal, *Insurgent Empire: Anticolonial Resistance and British Dissent* (London and New York: Verso, 2020).

chapter eight

1   Paul Kivel, *Boys Will Be Men: Raising Our Sons for Courage and Community* (Gabriola Island: New Society Publishers, 1999) and *Uprooting Racism: How White People Can Work for Racial Justice, Revised Edition* (Gabriola Island: New Society Publishers, 2002); Tim Wise, *White Like Me: Reflections on Race from a Privileged Son* (Brooklyn: Soft Skull Press, 2005); Robert Jensen, *The Heart of Whiteness: Confronting Race, Racism, and White Privilege* (San Francisco: City Lights Publishers, 2005); Inga Muscio, *Autobiography of a Blue-Eyed Devil: My Life and Times in a Racist, Imperialist Society* (Emeryville: Seal Press, 2005); Robin DiAngelo, *White Fragility: Why It's So Hard for White People to Talk about Racism* (Boston: Beacon Press, 2018); Fleming, *How to Be Less*; Oluo, *So You Want*; Layla F. Saad, *Me and White Supremacy: Combat Racism, Change the World, and Become a Good Ancestor* (Naperville: Sourcebooks, 2020); Ibram X. Kendi, *How to Be an Antiracist* (New York: One World, 2023).
2   Julietta Singh, *Unthinking Mastery: Dehumanism and Decolonial Entanglements* (Durham and London: Duke University Press, 2018), 27
3   Singh, *Unthinking Mastery*, 141. For decades, I have thought of part of my own process of taking up what I hear from others to understand them — as part of interpersonal relationships, but also as part of activism and organizing, and of writing — as "imaginative modelling." I think this is similar to what Singh means by "sympathetic imagination."
4   Singh, *Unthinking Mastery*, 24.
5   Singh, *Unthinking Mastery*, 139.
6   Robinson, *Hungry Listening*, 2.
7   Robinson, *Hungry Listening*, 53.
8   Robinson, *Hungry Listening*, 10.
9   Robinson, *Hungry Listening*, 10.

10 Robinson, *Hungry Listening*, 10–11.
11 Robinson, *Hungry Listening*, 39.
12 Harold Garfinkel, *Studies in Ethnomethodology* (Englewood Cliffs: Prentice-Hall, 1967); see also Frampton et al., *Sociology for Changing*.
13 Smith, "Political Activist as Ethnographer"; Frampton et al., *Sociology for Changing*; Aziz Choudry, *Learning Activism: The Intellectual Life of Contemporary Social Movements* (Toronto: University of Toronto Press, 2015); Aziz Choudry and Salim Vally (eds.), *Reflections on Knowledge, Learning and Social Movements: History's Schools* (New York: Routledge, 2019).
14 Scott Neigh, "Research in the Service of Struggle," *Talking Radical Radio* (podcast), December 7, 2021, talkingradical.ca/2021/12/07/radio-research-in-the-service-of-struggle/.
15 Douglas Bevington and Chris Dixon, "Movement-Relevant Theory: Rethinking Social Movement Scholarship and Activism," *Social Movement Studies* 4, 3 (2005), 185–208; Frampton et al., *Sociology for Changing*; Choudry, *Learning Activism*; Emily Brisette and Mike King, "Epistemologies of Struggle: Social Movement Theory and the Politics of Knowledge Production," *Humanity & Society* 47, 2 (2023), 1–15.
16 Scott Neigh, "Mapping and Opposing the Power of Fossil Fuel Industries in Canada," *Talking Radical Radio* (podcast), March 9, 2021, talkingradical.ca/2021/03/09/radio-mapping-and-opposing-the-power-of-fossil-fuel-industries-in-canada/
17 Scott Neigh, "A Successful Campaign Against Medical Colonialism," *Talking Radical Radio* (podcast), February 5, 2019, talkingradical.ca/2019/02/05/trr-hand_to_hold/; Samir Shaheen-Hussain, *Fighting for a Hand to Hold: Confronting Medical Colonialism Against Indigenous Children in Canada* (Montreal and Kingston: McGill-Queen's University Press, 2020); Scott Neigh, "The Past and Present of Medical Colonialism in Canada," *Talking Radical Radio* (podcast), March 2, 2021, talkingradical.ca/2021/03/02/radio-the-past-and-present-of-medical-colonialism-in-canada/.
18 A.K. Thompson, "Direct Action, Pedagogy of the Oppressed," in *Sociology for Changing the World: Social Movements/Social Research*, eds. Caelie Frampton et al. (Halifax: Fernwood Publishing, 2006), 99–118. The entire volume of Frampton et al. *Sociology for Changing* is worth reading on this point as well.
19 Thompson, "Direct Action," 99–105.
20 Thompson, "Direct Action," 105–07.
21 Smith, "Political Activist as Ethnographer"; see also Frampton et al., *Sociology for Changing* for some very useful discussion of this paper.
22 Smith, "Political Activist as Ethnographer," 44.
23 Frampton et al., *Sociology for Changing*; Agnieszka Doll, Laura Bisaillon, and Kevin Walby (eds.), *Political Activist Ethnography: Studies in the Social Relations of Struggle* (Athabasca AB: AU Press, 2024).
24 Choudry, *Learning Activism*.
25 Choudry, *Learning Activism*, 1.
26 Choudry, *Learning Activism*, 60.
27 Choudry, *Learning Activism*, 66.

28 Eve Kosofsky Sedgwick, "Paranoid Reading and Reparative Reading; or, You're So Paranoid, You Probably Think This Introduction Is About You," in *Novel Gazing: Queer Readings in Fiction*, ed. Eve Kosofsky Sedgwick (Durham and London: Duke University Press, 1997), 1–37.
29 Chris Dixon, "For the Long Haul: Building Social Movements with One Eye on the Past and the Other on the Future," *Briarpatch Magazine*, June 21, 2016, briarpatchmagazine.com/articles/view/for-the-long-haul.
30 Dixon, "For the Long Haul."
31 Choudry, *Learning Activism*; Scott Neigh, "Social Movements and How They Make, Learn, and Teach Ideas," *Talking Radical Radio* (podcast), January 20, 2016, talkingradical.ca/2016/01/20/trr-learning_activism/.
32 Shari Stone-Mediatore, *Reading Across Borders: Storytelling and Knowledges of Resistance* (New York: Palgrave Macmillan, 2003).
33 Stone-Meidatore, *Reading Across Borders*, 81.

conclusion

1 Though no doubt a world that enables greater emotional literacy and competency in all of us, but particularly in boys and men, might have led me to deal with that particular failure in a better way after the fact.
2 Glissant, *Poetics of Relation*.
3 Belcourt, *A History of My Brief Body*, 143.
4 Audra Simpson, *Mohawk Interruptus: Political Life Across the Borders of Settler States* (Durham: Duke University Press, 2014), 11.
5 Glissant, *Poetics of Relation*, 194.
6 Glissant, *Poetics of Relation*, 114.
7 Glissant, *Poetics of Relation*, 193.

epilogue

1 As US-based writer, organizer, and educator Walidah Imarisha writes, "Whenever we try to envision a world without war, without violence, without prisons, without capitalism, we are engaging in speculative fiction. All organizing is science fiction" ("Introduction," in *Octavia's Brood: Science Fiction Stories from Social Justice Movements*, eds. adrienne maree brown and Walidah Imarisha [Oakland and Edinburgh: AK Press, 2015], 3).
2 Angele Alook et al., *The End of This World: Climate Justice in So-Called Canada* (Toronto: Between the Lines, 2023).
3 For example, Natasha Lennard, "Liberals Rose to Fight the Assault on Abortion — but Not Trans Rights," *The Intercept*, December 31, 2022, theintercept.com/2022/12/31/trans-rights-abortion-liberals/.
4 Shane Burley (ed.), *¡No Pasarán! Antifascist Dispatches from a World in Crisis* (Chico: AK Press, 2022).
5 Shepard Fairey, "The Future Is Unwritten," *Huffpost*, November 15, 2011, www.huffpost.com/entry/new-york-city-homeless_b_1095462.
6 Rebecca Solnit, *Hope in the Dark: Untold Histories, Wild Possibilities*, Third Edition (Chicago: Haymarket Books, 2016), 109.

7   The online grassroots publication *The Breach* has given me the opportunity to write articles for them looking back at wins by social movements over each of the last few years. See Scott Neigh, "15 Movement Victories in 2021 You May Not Have Heard About," *The Breach*, January 6, 2022, breachmedia.ca/15-movement-victories-in-2021-you-may-not-have-heard-about/; "15 Movement Victories in 2022 You May Not Have Heard About," *The Breach*, December 22, 2022, breachmedia.ca/15-movement-victories-in-2022-you-may-not-have-heard-about/; "15 Movement Victories in 2023 You May Not Have Heard About," *The Breach*, December 21, 2023, breachmedia.ca/movement-victories-2023/; "15 movement victories in 2024 you may not have heard about," *The Breach*, December 20, 2024, breachmedia.ca/15-movement-victories-in-2024-you-may-not-have-heard-about/.

index

Abdillahi, Idil, 123
ableism, 3, 17, 26, 39, 79, 122
abolitionism, 37, 49, 103, 118, 121, 150
aboutness, 23–24
accounts of the social world, 40, 46–52, 55, 57–58, 139
   see also knowledge production, assessment of/during; knowledge production, and the social world
African Nova Scotians, 112–113, 121
Alinsky, Saul, 37
anarchism/anti-authoritarianism, 27, 54, 94, 106, 121
anti-colonial struggles
   challenging oppression in/by movements, 125
   collective struggle (examples), 65, 108–109, 117, 134, 145, 150
   and everyday resistance, 104
   and listening, 36–37
   and listening between movements, 118
anti-fascism, 37
anti-poverty struggles, 95, 109, 122
anti-racism/anti-racist struggles
   challenging oppression in/by movements, 123–123, 125
   critique of multiculturalism, 26
   collective struggle (examples), 49, 108–109, 112–113, 114, 117, 134, 145
   everyday resistance (examples), 97–98, 99–100, 103, 105
   and intersectionality, 54
   and listening between movements, 118–120, 121
   resources (anti-racism/anti-oppression), 127–128, 131
   and standpoint, 28, 76
anti-war struggles, 109

armed struggle, 109–110, 168n17
As We Have Always Done (Simpson), 104
attention, 4, 18–19, 23–24, 29, 51, 74–76, 142–143

Bayat, Asef, 100–101, 105
Belcourt, Billy-Ray, 46, 146
Black Feminist Thought (Hill Collins), 99–100
Black freedom struggle,
   challenging oppression in/by movements, 123–125
   collective struggle (examples), 49, 109, 112–113, 114, 145, 159–160n20
   everyday resistance (examples), 97–98, 99–100, 103, 105
   and intersectionality, 54, 159–160n20
   and listening between movements, 118, 119, 120, 121, 169n25
   and standpoint, 28
BlackLife (Walcott and Abdillahi), 123
Black Reconstruction in America (Du Bois), 95
Black Test, 123–124
Boggs, Grace Lee, 95
breaching experiments, 132
brown, adrienne maree, 37
Bush, George W., 81

Cabral, Amilcar, 36–37
Camfield, David, 42–43
capitalism, 26, 39, 54, 60, 87, 137, 145, 150, 161n2
   and knowledge production, 43–45
   see also hegemony; specific oppressions
characteristics of the social world (useful in knowledge production), 52–53, 142
Choudry, Aziz, 136, 137, 139

circulation of struggle, 118–119, 168n22
cissexism, *see* transphobia
Clash, The, 151
classism, 77
climate crisis/movement, 65, 134, 150, 152
Cloward, Richard, 95
collectivity, 7, 9–10, 110–114, 167n13
colonialism
    and everyday life, 70
    and everyday resistance, 104
    examples of, 7, 39, 65, 81, 91, 120, 150
    and listening/knowledge production, 26, 83–86, 130, 141, 143–145, 164n4
    and liberalism, 45
    and social movements, 108, 134
    see also anti-colonial struggles; Indigenous peoples/struggles
Combahee River Collective, 54
communities-in-struggle
    definition of, 7
    see also social movements
complexity
    as barrier to knowledge production, 42–43, 49–50, 137
    as feature of the social world, 41, 53, 129–130
    of listening, 20–21, 66–70, 129–130, 140–142
Coombs, Loni, 30
Coulthard, Glen, 104
Crenshaw, Kimberlé, 54
critical listening positionality, 130–131
    see also standpoint
culture
    and everyday resistance, 96
    of individualism, *see* individualism
    and listening, 16–17, 25–26, 29, 72, 80, 156n1

The Dawn of Everything (Graeber and Wengrow), 27
Deafness, 3, 17
Decolonizing Methodologies (Smith), 83–84, 86
dehumanization
    and knowledge production, 84–86, 137, 138
    see also oppression (in general); specific oppressions
direct action, 51–52, 108–109, 116, 117–118
    and knowledge production, 134–136, 139
disability, *see* ableism
Dixon, Chris, 138–139
doctrine of discovery, 81
Donne, John, 39
Dr. Phil (Phillip McGraw), 30
Du Bois, W.E.B., 95

eating the Other, 86
Engels, Friederich, 45
enlarged thought, 141
environmental struggles, 109, 134, 150, 152
epistemology, *see* knowledge production
eros effect, 168n22
Escher, M.C., 42
ethnomethodology, 132
everyday compliance, 92–94, 107
everyday complicity, 92, 112
everyday living, 92–94
everyday participation, 91–2
everyday resistance, 6, 92–106, 107, 109, 110, 112, 122, 123, 151, 164n4, 165n1
    and knowledge production, 132–133, 136, 142–143
    limits as a framework, 104, 105
    limits of, 105–106
    moralizing about, 94, 97, 102
    overlap with everyday compliance and everyday living, 93
    in relational context, 103–104
everyday solidarity, 92, 112

far right, 7, 47, 116, 150–151
Featherstone, David, 119–120
features of the social world (useful in knowledge production), 52–53, 142
feminism, 46, 75–76, 145, 151, 159–160n20
    challenging oppression in/by movements, 124
    collective struggle (examples), 103, 110, 121

everyday resistance (examples), 99–100, 101
and intersectionality, 54, 159–160n20
and listening between movement, 169n25
and listening/knowledge production, 37, 55–58, 127
and standpoint, 28
Fleming, Crystal, 75, 76
Floyd, George, 188
Freire, Paulo, 19

Garfinkel, Harold, 132
gay struggles, *see* 2SLGBTQI+ struggles
gender oppression, *see* sexism
Glissant, Éduoard, 86, 146
good listener, 80
Goulston, Mark, 81
Graeber, David, 27
Graham, Rev. Billy, 81
Gramsci, Antonio, 27
Gray, Jim, 30

harm, *see* oppression (in general); listening, and harm; social movements, harm caused in/by; specific oppressions
Hayes, Kelly, 37, 76
hearing, 15
  versus listening, 3, 4, 15, 17, 32
  versus vision, 15–16
hegemony, 26–27, 44, 74, 75, 97
heterosexism/homophobia, 26, 44, 81, 91, 122
  Toronto bathhouse raids, 135, 137, 140–141
Hill Collins, Patricia, 54, 99–100, 159n20, 160n29
history
  and knowledge production, 140
  and listening, 16, 83–86
  and social movements, 111, 120–121
HIV/AIDS movement, 135
Holloway, John, 60–61, 153n5, 161n2
homelessness, 63, 109, 145, 148–149
hooks, bell, 75–76, 86
hope, 7, 151–152
How Leaders Speak (Gray), 30

How to Talk to Anyone (Lowndes), 30
hungry listening, 86, 130, 147
Hunt-Hendrix, Leah, 37

Idle No More, 114
imagination, 34
  sympathetic, 129
Indigenous peoples/struggles
  collective struggle (examples), 109, 112–113, 114, 117, 123, 124, 134, 150
  everyday resistance (examples), 104
  and listening/knowledge production, 26, 36, 37, 83–85, 127, 130–131, 141, 156n1
  and standpoint, 35, 52, 75
indignity, *see* oppression (in general); listening, and harm; social movements, harm caused in/by; specific oppressions
individualism, 2, 9–10, 32, 44–46, 49, 82, 106, 111
injustice, *see* oppression (in general); specific oppressions
innocence, claims of, 10, 92
institutional ethnography, 55–57, 160n25
International Working Men's Association, 120
intersectionality/interconnection, 54, 63, 71, 124, 159n20

James, C.L.R., 95
Just Listen (Goulston), 81

Kaba, Mariame, 37, 55
Kant, Immanuel, 141
Katsiaficas, George, 118–119, 168n22
Kelley, Robin D.G., 97–99, 103, 105, 106
Kinsman, Gary, 120–121, 160n25
knowledge production, 2, 5, 6, 8–9, 12, 20–28, 35, 47–58, 126–143, 155n18, 156n1
  anti-racism/anti-oppression resources, 127–128
  assessment of/during, 20–21, 23–25, 47–58, 133, 136–143
  beyond the immediate, 33, 63–71, 149
  colonialism, 83–86, 130, 144–145, 164n4

culture, 25–26, 156n1
dehumanization, 84–86, 137, 138
direct action, 134–136, 139
everyday resistance, 132–133, 136, 142–143
experience, 40–42, 50–52, 57, 70, 139, 160n29
kinds within movements, 139–140
limits of, 40, 42–46, 47, 49–50, 64–65, 83–86, 143–145
more, 33, 63–71, 149
schemas/scripts, 21, 24, 26, 27, 76
scholarly resources, 128–131, 132
social movements, 2, 6, 8, 10, 12, 46, 108, 116, 127–143, 145–147, 154n13, 168n17
stories, 139–143
and the social world, 2, 39–58, 63–71, 74–78, 83–86
theory/investigation, 10, 51, 52, 53–58, 65, 70–71, 154n13
universities, 46–47
see also listening; standpoint

labour movement, *see* worker exploitation/struggles
language, 5, 17, 20, 22, 24, 109, 142
LGBT struggles, *see* 2SLGBTQI+ struggles
liberalism, 2, 45, 49
Life as Politics (Bayat), 100–101, 105
listening
  as active, 3–4, 18–22, 27–28
  advice, 29–32, 51–58, 126–131, 136–139, 140–143, 149
  assumed to be good, 78–82
  beyond the immediate, 33, 63–71, 149
  definition of, 2–4, 15–17, 156n1
  in everyday life, 1–2, 4–6, 12, 14–15, 17–19, 33–35, 60–71, 148–149, 152
  as everyday resistance, 100
  failures of, 6, 64–65, 67–68, 72–74, 77–78, 82–87, 143–147, 162n12
  to the future, 149–151
  and harm, 6, 16, 17, 72, 74–87, 91, 137, 143–147, 162n11
  versus hearing, 3, 4, 15, 17, 32

as individual, 6, 9–10, 29, 32, 38, 58, 82–83, 126–127, 147, 149
as interpersonal/intersubjective, 6, 12, 16, 29, 32–36, 38, 58, 65–71, 117, 147
learning how, 22–25, 27–28, 51, 74–77, 82
models of, 19–22
more, 33, 63–71, 149
to the past, 120–121
pleasures of, 36
and power, 6, 26–28, 86–88, 100, 127–131, 144–147
practices, 19–26, 76, 126–131
and proximity, 18–19
as social, 16, 38, 39, 58, 126, 149
and social movements, 1, 4, 6, 8–9, 10–11, 12, 29, 36–38, 87–88, 116–125, 131–143, 145–147, 149, 151–152
and social organization, 58, 64–65, 72, 74–78, 82–88, 144–145, 149
see also knowledge production
lobbying, 108
Lorde, Audre, 54
The Lost Art of Good Conversation (Mipham), 82
Lukács, Georg, 43
Luxemburg, Rosa, 95

Marcuse, Herbert, 168n22
marginal experience narratives, 142–143
  see also knowledge production, everyday resistance; knowledge production, social movements
Marshall, John, 81
Marx, Karl, 16, 43, 45, 46, 55
Marxism, 37, 43, 49–50, 95
matrix of domination, 54
Maynard, Robyn, 85
McDonald's restaurants, 99, 103
McKittrick, Katherine, 85
media (grassroots), 8, 117, 152
meetings (as social movement practice), 108
memory, 21, 34, 140

microaggressions, 79–80
migrant justice, 37, 109, 111, 145
Mipham, Sakyong, 82
Mishra, Pankaj, 45
Montgomery, Nick, 138
more, 33, 63–71, 149
murmur, 60–62, 65, 68, 77, 90, 147, 148

Nawrocki, Norman, 37
neoliberalism, 9, 45, 82, 106, 113
neurodivergence, 3
nonmovements, 105
   see also everyday resistance
non-profit industrial complex, 122
noticing, 17–19, 23–24, 75–77
Novick, Michael, 37

objectification, 16, 17, 84, 86
Occupy, 114
opacity, 146
oppression (in general), 7, 26, 39, 53–54, 56, 60–63, 65, 68–70, 74–88, 112–113, 121–125, 127–131, 137–138, 142–143, 144–146, 150–152, 162n11
   challenging within movements, 124–125
   individualist responses to, 9–10, 83, 127–128
   moments of, 90–94, 95, 101–103, 132–133
   see also privilege; specific oppressions
organizing
   limits as a framework, 115, 168n16
   as science fiction, 172n1 (epilogue)
   see also social movements; specific struggles
Orientalism (Said), 83–84, 86
Orwell, George, 94
out-of-placeness, 23–24, 76–77

Palestinian struggle, 114, 145, 151
Palmater, Pamela, 36
Pannekoek, Anton, 95
paranoid reading/listening, 138–139
patriarchy, *see* sexism
peace movement, *see* anti-war struggles

peasant struggles, 94–97, 105
Piven, Frances Fox, 95
policing, 42, 49, 51–52, 56–57, 69, 101, 108, 114, 118, 135, 137, 139, 149, 150
political activist ethnography, 135–136, 139
political parties, 122–123
poverty
   gas station example, 63–65, 97
   homelessness, 109, 145, 148–149
   social assistance system, 56, 86
   see also anti-poverty struggles; peasant struggles; worker exploitation/struggles
Prashad, Vijay, 37
praxis, 134
privilege
   and everyday complicity, 92
   and listening, 10, 51–52, 74–77, 86, 128, 131
   and resistance, 94, 102, 109
   see also oppression (in general); specific oppressions; standpoint
protest, 17, 107, 110, 112, 114, 117
   see also social movements; specific struggles
proximity, 18–19
purity politics, 11, 123

Race Rebels (Kelley), 97–99, 105
racial justice, *see* anti-racism/anti-racist struggles
racism
   and everyday life, 69–70, 92, 162n11
   and everyday resistance, 97–98, 99–100, 105
   and listening, 74–77, 83–86, 137
   policing, 52, 56–57
   resources (anti-racism/anti-oppression), 9, 127–128
   and social movements, 122, 123–125, 137
   see also anti-colonial struggles; anti-racism/anti-racist struggles; Black freedom struggle; Indigenous struggles; oppression (in general)

Rebick, Judy, 37
reification, 43, 46, 55, 75
relations of ruling, 56
reparative reading/listening, 138–139
research (as part of struggle), 84, 108, 116, 133–134, 136
   see also knowledge production
resistance (as collective activity), 7, 110–114, 167n13
   see also everyday resistance; protest; social movements; specific tactics
revolution, 102, 109–110
Robinson, Dylan, 86, 130–131
Rumsfeld, Donald, 81

Said, Edward, 83–84, 86
schemas and scripts, 21, 24, 26, 27, 76
Scott, James. C., 93–97, 164n4
scream, 60–62, 65, 68, 77, 90, 147, 148, 161n2 (chap. 4)
Sedgwick, Eve Kosofsky, 138
segregation, 97–98, 103
self-formation, 4–6, 14–15, 25–28, 34–35, 39, 41–42, 48, 71, 127, 155n18
self-improvement, 9, 11, 29–31, 82–83, 147, 149
   see also listening, advice
senses, 3–4, 15–17, 20, 22, 153n1
   biology of, 15, 22, 155n12
   impairment, 3
   see also Deafness; hearing; vision
sexism
   in everyday life, 62, 66–67, 68–69, 79, 80, 82, 91, 162n11
   and everyday resistance, 99–100, 105
   and listening, 16, 73–74, 76–77, 77–78
   resources (anti-racism/anti-oppression), 127
   and social movements, 121–122, 124, 137
Shaffir, Rebecca, 81
Sharpe, Christina, 70
Simpson, Audra, 146
Simpson, Leanne Betasamosake, 36, 104, 124
Singh, Julietta, 128–129, 131

slavery, 97, 100, 103, 120
Smith, Dorothy, 55–58, 135, 160n25
Smith, George, 135, 137, 140
Smith, Kim, 138
Smith, Linda Tuhiwai, 83–84, 86
socialism, 44–45, 121
social media, 24, 33–34, 69, 86, 116, 117
social movements, 6–7, 36–37, 45, 90–91, 106, 107–125, 151–152
   challenging oppression within, 124–125
   definition of, 7
   education as part of, 108, 117–118
   harm caused in/by, 102–103, 121–125, 137, 153n5
   impacts of, 117–118
   and knowledge production, 2, 6, 8, 10, 12, 46, 108, 116, 127–143, 145–147, 154n13, 168n17
   listening and, 1, 4, 6, 8–9, 10–11, 12, 29, 36–38, 87–88, 116–125, 131–143, 145–147, 149, 151–152
   meetings as part of, 108
   in the Middle East, 100–101, 103, 105
   reconfigured relationships and, 110–115, 124
   work involved in, 113–117
   see also protest; specific movements/struggles; specific tactics
social organization, 2, 5, 16, 28, 39–58, 91, 111–112, 145
   characteristics of relevant to knowledge production, 52–54
   of forgetting, 120–121
   and listening, 58, 64–65, 72, 74–78, 82–88, 144–145, 149
   see also accounts of the social world; knowledge production, and the social world; specific social relations of oppression
solidarity, 37, 68, 94, 98, 146, 147
   everyday, 92, 112
   between social movements, 119–120
Solidarity (Featherstone), 119–120
Solnit, Rebecca, 151
standpoint, 35, 47, 70–71, 127, 140–141, 149
   definition and origins, 28

Dorothy Smith's usage, 56–57
and failures/harms of listening 74–78, 82–88
formed through experience, 28, 74–77, 132
and out-of-placeness, 76
see also critical listening positionality; knowledge production, limits of; listening, and harm; listening, failures of; marginal experience narratives
Sterne, Jonathan, 15–17, 24
Stoever, Jennifer Lynn, 100
Stone-Mediatore, Shari, 140–142
stories (in knowledge production), 139–143
Strummer, Joe, 151
synesthesia, 153n1

Talking Radical Radio, 8–9, 152, 153n10
Taylor, Astra, 37
Taylor, Keeanga-Yamahtta, 159–160n20
tenant struggles, 112, 113, 114, 137
Tennyson, Alfred Lord, 39
Thompson, E.P., 94–95
transformative justice organizing, 103
transparency, 86, 146, 147
transphobia, 7, 77, 91, 123, 151
Trump, Donald, 151, 167n13
2SLGBTQI+ struggles
harms within movements, 122, 123, 124
and listening/knowledge production, 135, 137, 140
collective (examples), 102, 145, 151

Upping the Anti, 154n13

Van Meter, Kevin, 122
Vietnam War, 118–119
vision, 15–16
vulnerable reading/listening, 128–129

Walcott, Rinaldo, 123
Walia, Harsha, 37, 111
Walmart, 81

Walton, Sam, 81
Weapons of the Weak (Scott), 94–97
Weber, Max, 46
Wengrow, David, 27
We'tsuwe'ten people, 114
white supremacy, *see* racism
worker exploitation/struggles
collective struggle (examples), 102, 107–108, 112, 118, 119, 120, 145
everyday resistance (examples), 95, 97, 99, 103
experiences of exploitation, 60, 68, 81, 91, 93
gas station example, 63–65, 97
and harm in social movements, 122
Wynter, Sylvia, 85–86

Zapatistas, 62
The Zen of Listening (Shafir), 81